Science
Olympiad

Class 05

A must have book for all
Olympiads & Talent Search Exams...

by
Satyam Kumar Soni

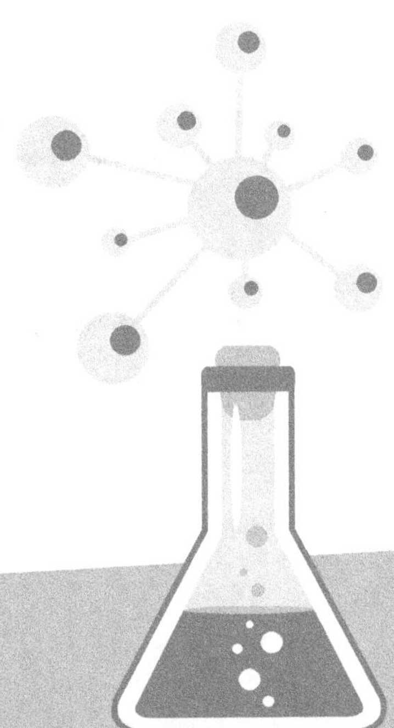

BLOOM CAP
Bloom Cap Edu Ventures Pvt. Ltd.

Bloom Cap Edu Ventures Pvt. Ltd.

卐 **Administrative & Production Office**

'Ramchhaya' 4577/15, Agarwal Road, Darya Ganj, New Delhi -110002
Tele: 011- 47630600, 43518550

卐 **ISBN :** 978-93-25519-34-3

卐 **PRICE :** ₹100.00

卐 **PO No :** TXT-XX-XXXXXXX-X-XX

For further information about the books log on to
www.bloomcap.org

Follow us on   

Preface

"Future belongs to those Who prepares for it today"

School Olympiads are National & International level competitions conducted by different Government, Non-Government & Educational Organisations with the purpose of making the children ready to face competitive exams.

The challenging Questions asked in Olympiads motivate them to learn more & more and bring out the best result with improved academic performance. The Awards & Scholarship offered by Olympiads motivate children to aspire & strive for doing better and emerge out to be the best.

Science Olympiads

Being a Scientist or Engineer or Doctor has always been a dream of each school going child. A good command over Science is a must for any of these. Questions of Science Olympiads are structured to help students to develop scientific temperament & motivate them to understand the concepts of science. They also focuses on improving existing knowledge of a student by adding more information.

'Bloom Science Olympiad Study Book Class 5' is a perfect resource to Study & Practice for Olympiad Exams and other National & State Level Talent Search Exams & Other Competitions.

Some Special Features of Bloom Science Olympiad Study Books are;

- Chapterwise Exercises having different types of Objective Questions; Analytical, Applications, Remembering etc, at par with the Olympiad Level.
- Detailed Explanation for each question.
- Olympiad Pattern Practice Sets at the end.

This book is prepared by Expert Panel with the utmost care, still if you have any suggestions regarding its improvement then feel free to contact us at olympiads@bloomcap.org. We will try to inculcate your suggestions in the further editions.

Contents

Chapter 01

Animals

1 Mark Questions

1. Which of these animals have shell as the outer covering?
   (a) Mice   (b) Prawn
   (c) Mosquito   (d) Lizard

2. The wings of the birds are their
   (a) separate structure (b) hindlimbs
   (c) forelimbs   (d) None of these

3. Which of the following has the most extreme sense of hearing?

(a)

(b)

(c)

(d)

4. Part *A* is essential in aiding the movement in penguins. Which option correctly identifies it?

(a) Webbed feet   (b) Fins
(c) Flippers   (d) Oars

5. Siberian cranes, eels, butterflies and Arctic tern.
   A feature common to all these organisms is that they are all
   (a) aerial animals
   (b) exhibit migration during cold weather
   (c) herbivores
   (d) oviparous

6. The animals which can live both in water and on land are called
   (a) reptiles   (b) mammals
   (c) aquatic   (d) amphibians

7. Which of the following does not have fur on its body?
   (a) Yak
   (b) Sheep
   (c) Mountain goat
   (d) Fish

8. Which of the following animals can be removed from the row when classification is done with respect to feeding habits?

(I)

(II)

(III)

(IV)

(a) I and II   (b) II and III
(c) I and IV   (d) III and IV

9. Which of the following option a pair of has animals that move in same way?
(a) Shark and lizard
(b) Zebra and lizard
(c) Crow and caterpillar
(d) Bear and snake

10. Which among the following is not a feature of desert plants?
(a) Small leaves
(b) Spine
(c) Sloping branches
(d) Thick stems

11. The columns A, B and C shows the animals, body coverings and functions performed by them. Select the option which correctly matches the columns.

	Column A (Animals)	Column B (Body covering)	Column C (Functions)
(a)		Spines	Keeps the body warm
(b)		Shell	Protect from injuries
(c)		Feathers	Protection from predators
(d)		Fur	Helps in flight

12. How does an eagle flying high in the sky notice its prey on the ground?
(a) Strong sense of smell
(b) Strong eyesight
(c) Strong sense of hearing
(d) Strong sense of taste

13. The animal 'A' can sense his female mate kilometres away from him. It also makes a natural protein fibre, some forms of which can be woven into textiles. Who is it?
(a) Silkworm   (b) Butterfly
(c) Moth   (d) Earthworm

14. There are so many animals who hunt their prey, so as to obtain food. Do you know among them tigers hunt during night? What could be the reason for this?
(a) They just like to roam around and hunt in night
(b) Their sight is six times better than humans during night
(c) Number of preys are less during daytime due to heat
(d) They do not want to share their food with any other animal

15. What advantage do birds have of having eyes on either side of their head?
(a) They can focus on two different things at one time
(b) They can occasionally give rest to one of their eyes
(c) They look beautiful with such eyes
(d) They can fly better

2 Marks Questions

16. To hide from predators some animals protect themselves by blending its colour similar to its surroundings.

This phenomenon is shown by *Chameleon*.

Among the colours mentioned below, a *Chameleon* while walking on grass will use which one, in case a predators is coming near?

(a) Brown   (b) Green

(c) Yellow   (d) Red

17. Study the given flow chart and identify the labels X, Y and Z.

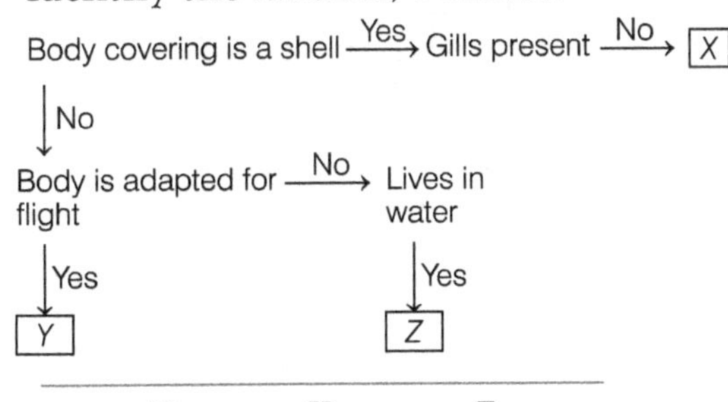

	X	Y	Z
(a)	Fish	Prawn	Snake
(b)	Bird	Fish	Lizard
(c)	Snail	Bird	Fish
(d)	Frog	Bird	Fish

18. Mosquito can find us by

(a) Heat of our body

(b) Smell of our body

(c) Sound of our body

(d) Movement of our body

19. Read the following statements carefully and choose the correct option.

Statement I All the birds can fly.

Statement II Dolphins communicate using ultrasound.

(a) Statements I and II are false

(b) Statement I is false

(c) All statements are true

(d) All statements are false

20. Ants moves in a line because of their sense of

(a) sight   (b) smell

(c) taste   (d) hearing

Plants

1 Mark Questions

1. Vegetative propagation involves the production of new plants from which part of parent plants?
   (a) Stems, leaves and flowers
   (b) Stems, roots and leaves
   (c) Stems, flowers and fruits
   (d) Stems, roots and flowers

2. Identify the process represented by the figure shown below.

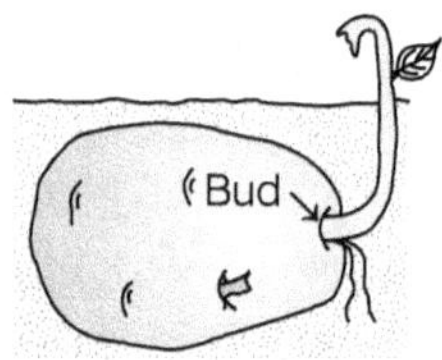

   (a) Fertilisation
   (b) Pollination
   (c) Vegetative propagation
   (d) Dispersion

3. Which part of the rose plant can grow into new plants?
   (a) Roots   (b) Flowers
   (c) Stem   (d) Seeds

4. Where does the food comes from when a young seed has not yet grown its leaves?
   (a) From air   (b) From soil
   (c) From cotyledons (d) From other trees

5. Seeds are found in the ...... which are developed from the ....
   (a) fruits; flowers
   (b) flowers; fruits
   (c) leaves; fruits
   (d) fruits; leaves

6. In the given diagram, label A, B and C are

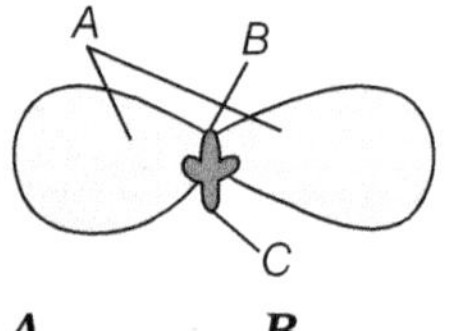

       A   **B**   **C**
   (a) Tiny shoot, Tiny root, Cotyledon
   (b) Cotyledon, Tiny shoot, Tiny root
   (c) Tiny root, Cotyledon, Tiny shoot
   (d) Tiny root, Tiny shoot, Cotyledon

7. Complete the following diagram and choose the correct option for X and Y

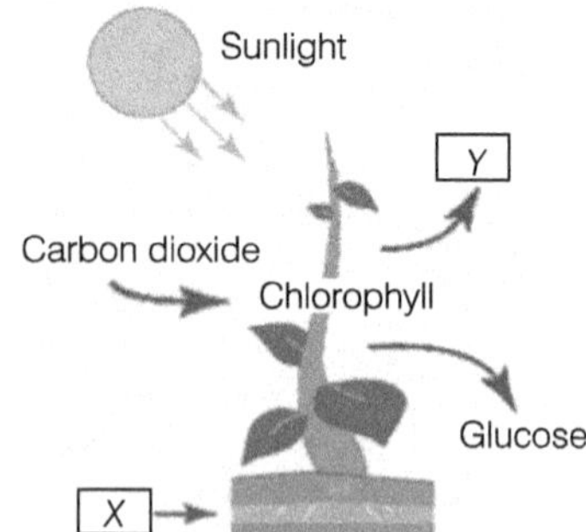

	X	Y
(a)	Oxygen	Water
(b)	Water	Oxygen
(c)	Oxygen	Nitrogen
(d)	Nitrogen	Oxygen

8. Complete the following diagram, depicting four major agents of dispersal of seeds.

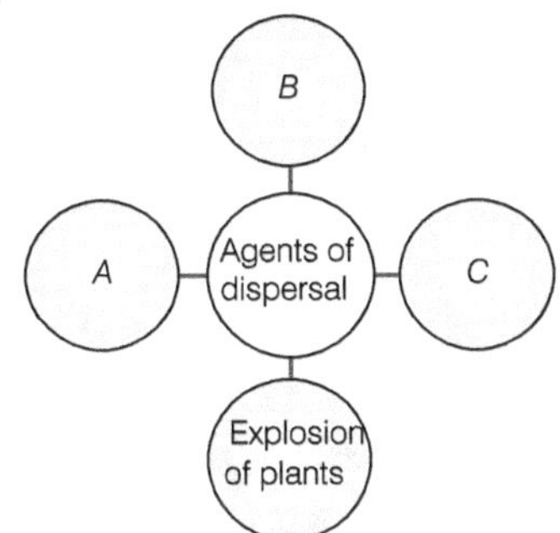

	A	B	C
(a)	Wind	Water	Animals
(b)	Sun	Tree	Hand picking
(c)	Wind	Water	Sun
(d)	Water	Animals	Tree

9. Match the following columns.

Column I	Column II
A. Dispersal	1. Production of new plants from parents
B. Germination	2. Carrying of seeds away from their parent plant
C. Reproduction	3. Development of seed into seedling

Codes

	A	B	C			A	B	C
(a)	1	2	3		(b)	3	1	2
(c)	2	1	3		(d)	2	3	1

10. Identify the name of an insectivorous plant
(a) *Cactus*   (b) Lotus
(c) Money plant   (d) Pitcher plant

11. The seed in the figure given below being dispersed by animal will have which of the following characteristics?

   I. Light weight
  II. Sticky texture
 III. Spine-like structures on surface

Choose the correct option.
(a) I and II   (b) II and III
(c) Only II   (d) I and III

12. Study the given flow chart.

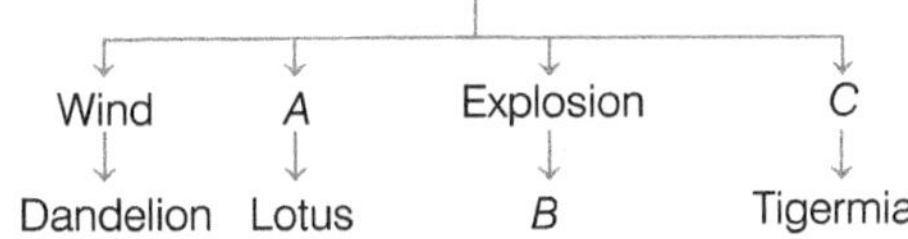

(a) *A* - Wind, *B* - Milk weed, *C* - Animals
(b) *A* - Water, *B* - *Cactus*, *C* - Explosion
(c) *A* - Wind, *B* - Pea, *C* - Water
(d) *A* - Water, *B* - Pea, *C* - Animals

13. Study the following statements and choose the correct option.Where [F] represents false and [T] represents true statement.

   I. Plants do not play any role to decrease soil erosion.
  II. All the seeds do not grow into a new plant.
 III. Air is not essential for seeds to grow.
 IV. Plants are the only producer of food on Earth.

Codes

	I	II	III	IV
(a)	F	T	F	T
(b)	T	T	F	F
(c)	F	F	T	T
(d)	T	F	T	F

14. Mihika bought some lemon seeds. She put them in a pot, watered them and kept them in the refrigerator. After going out of station for a few days, she came back home. She checked her pot in the fridge. She found that....... .

(a) her lemon plant had a shoot
(b) her lemon plant had lemons on it
(c) it had not grown at all as it had no warmth and sunlight
(d) it was just germination

15. How onion and ginger are related to each other?

(a) Leaves of both can grow into new plants
(b) They are underground stems from which new plants grow
(c) Roots of both can grow into new plants
(d) Both are dispersed by explosive mechanism

16. Four friends A, B, C and D have prepared a set up for observing germination of seeds, The set ups are shown below.

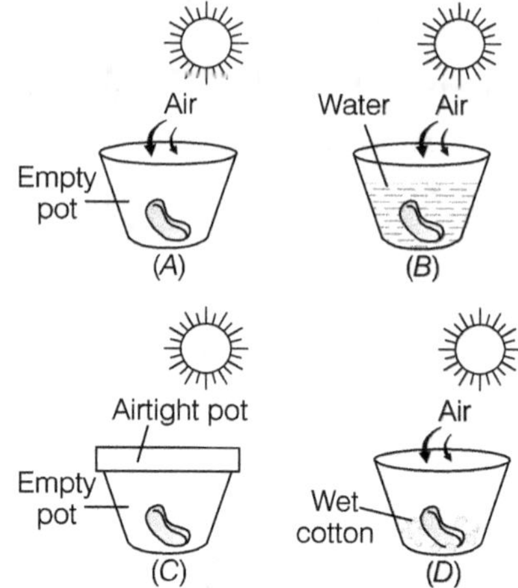

Which experimental set up will yield positive results?

(a) A and B (b) Only A
(c) C and D (d) Only D

2 Marks Questions

17. The table given below classifies some plants according to their use.

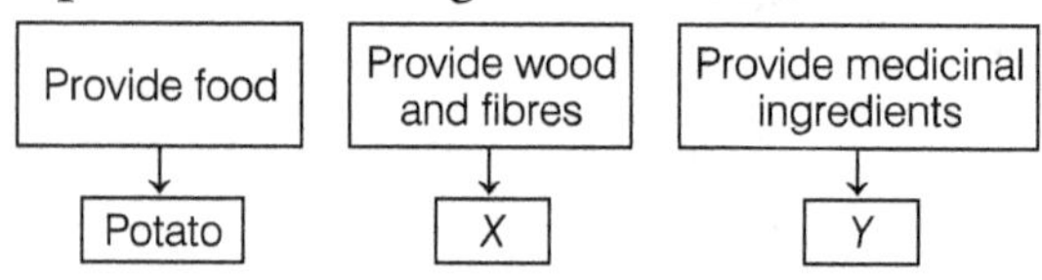

Which one of the following plant pairs should be used for X and Y ?

(a) X - Teak, Y - Sugarcane
(b) X - Bamboo, Y - Aloe vera
(c) X - Garlic, Y - Coconut
(d) X - Coconut, Y - Teak

18. Diagram below shows a young plant. The seed leaves of this plant become smaller as the plant grows bigger. This is because......... .

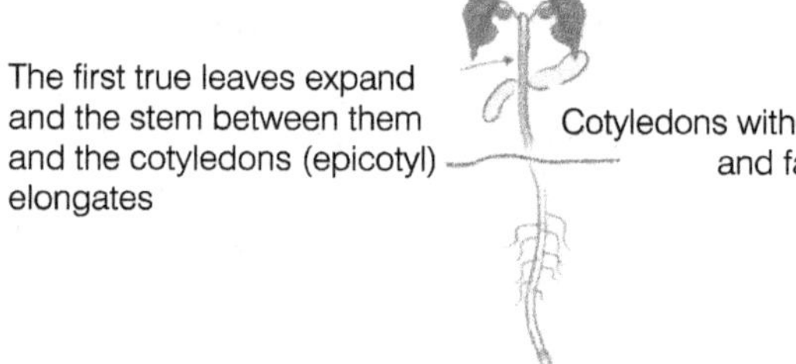

(a) sunlight dries the seed leaves
(b) the seed leaves are absorbed back into the seed coat
(c) the seed leaves perform photosynthesis in the presence of sunlight
(d) the food from the seed leaves has been used by the plants

19. The plant X has both medicinal as well as religious value. Choose the correct option for plant X.
(a) Marigold
(b) Tea
(c) Aloe vera
(d) Tulsi

20. Match the Column I with Column II.

	Column I		Column II
A.	The process by which plants make food	1.	Pollination
B.	The process of transfer of pollen grain from anther to stigma	2.	Seed dispersal
C.	Scattering of seed	3.	Germination
D.	The process of growth plant from a seed	4.	Photosynthesis

Codes

	A	B	C	D		A	B	C	D
(a)	3	4	1	2	(b)	4	1	2	3
(c)	4	1	3	2	(d)	3	4	2	1

21. Study the given diagram and answer the following question.

What will happen if seeds are sown so much close to one another?
(a) They will grow in normal manner
(b) They will fight for nutrients, space and sunlight
(c) They will support each other growth
(d) They will give high yield to the farmers

Human Body and Its Functioning

1 Mark Questions

1. I am a component of skeletal system who protects brain. 22 bones are involved in forming my shell-like structure. Who am I?

(a) Ribcage (b) Spine (c) Skull (d) Girdles

2. Which of the following movement does not involve the use of joints?

(a) The nodding of head
(b) The blinking of eyes
(c) The bending of fingers
(d) Kneeling down

3. Refer to the given relationship and select the option which correctly identifies X

Gliding joint: Wrist :: ...... : Knees
(a) Pivot joint   (b) Fixed joint
(c) Hinge joint   (d) Ball and socket joint

4. Which of the following is incorrect regarding the parts labelled A, B, C and D

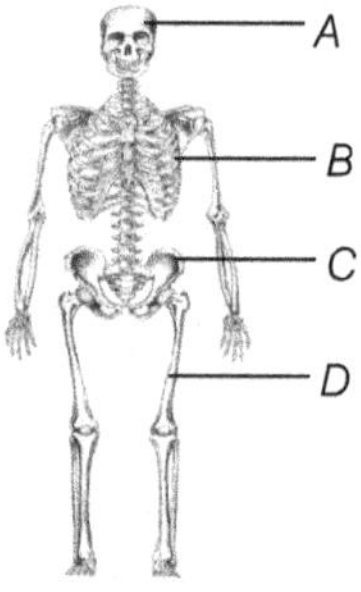

(a) A - Protects the brain
(b) B - Protects heart and lungs
(c) C - Protects spinal cord
(d) D - Longest bone of the body

5. Mohit met with an accident and had a fracture. Which of the following clearly gives the details of the fracture to the doctor?

(a) Blood report   (b) An X-ray
(c) Muscle test   (d) Urine report

6. Refer to the classification table

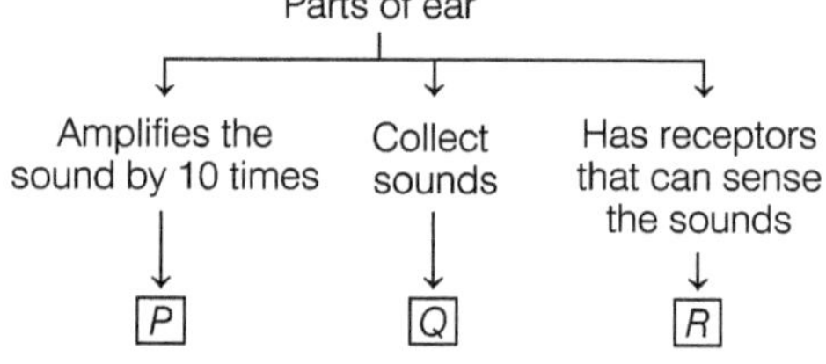

Select the correct option to identify P, Q and R

(a) P - Outer ear, Q - Inner ear, R -Middle ear
(b) P - Middle ear, Q - Inner ear, R - Outer ear
(c) P - Outer ear, Q - Middle ear, R - Inner ear
(d) P - Middle ear, Q - Outer ear, R - Inner ear

7. Read the following statements and choose the incorrect statement.
 (a) Wash the eyes often with hot water
 (b) We should not read in a moving vehicle
 (c) Use clean towel and clean hands, while touching the eyes
 (d) Get regular eye check up done

8. Match the following columns.

	Column I		Column II
A.	Digestion	1.	Kidneys
B.	Circulation	2.	Lungs
C.	Excretion	3.	Stomach
D.	Respiration	4.	Heart

Codes

	A	B	C	D		A	B	C	D
(a)	1	2	3	4	(b)	2	3	1	4
(c)	3	4	1	2	(d)	4	1	2	3

9. Neck of giraffe is much longer than ours, rather it has longest neck. Does neck of giraffe has more number of vertebrae than our neck? Give reason.
 (a) Yes, because it has so long neck
 (b) No, neck is long because of longer vertebrae. Number is same
 (c) Yes, because it is a large animal
 (d) No, rather it has big bundles of muscles in between

10. What enables us to swing our arms as shown in the picture?

 (a) Ball and socket joint
 (b) Pivot joint
 (c) Hinge joint
 (d) Sliding joint

11. The controlling center of our body is
 (a) heart
 (b) brain
 (c) kidney
 (d) stomach

12. Which type of stimulus is not generally detected by our skin?
 (a) Heat   (b) Pain
 (c) Cold   (d) Light

13. Which muscle matched correctly with their diagram?

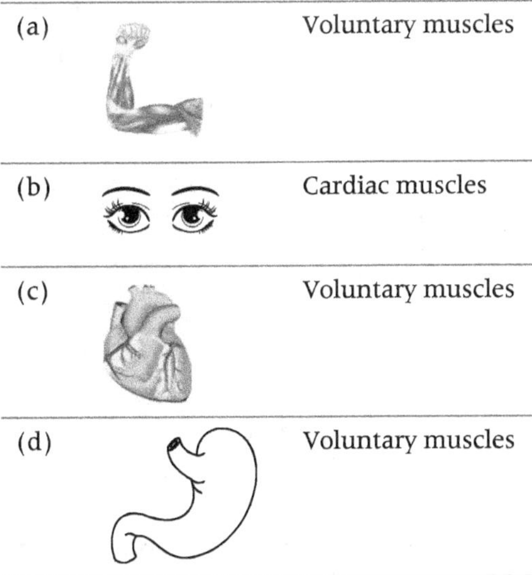

(a)	Voluntary muscles
(b)	Cardiac muscles
(c)	Voluntary muscles
(d)	Voluntary muscles

14. On eating rice in a meal, we get a sweet after taste in our mouth. The most suitable explanation for this is
 (a) carbohydrates in rice changed to sugar
 (b) proteins in rice changes to sugar
 (c) rice is sweet in taste change
 (d) fats in rice change to starch during digestion

2 Marks Questions

15. Refer to the flow chart given below choose the correct option for *P-Q*

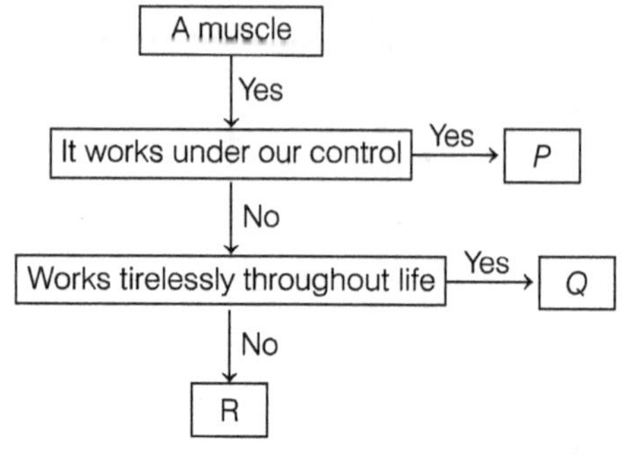

	P	*Q*	*R*
(a)	Kidney	Hands	Brain
(b)	Legs	Heart	Lungs
(c)	Legs	Hands	Stomach
(d)	Brain	Kidney	Heart

16. Which of the following organs are found in pairs?

(i) Lung   (ii) Heart

(iii) Kidney   (iv) Stomach

(v) Food pipe   (vi) Brain

(a) (i), (iii) and (v)

(b) (ii), (v) and (vi)

(c) (i) and (iii)

(d) Only (iii)

17. Choose the incorrect match from the following option.

(a) Number of the teeth in adults = 32

(b) Number of bones in adults = 206

(c) Number of ribs in adults = 24

(d) Number of bones in skull = 33

18. Your mouth waters even if you hear name of your favourite food. Some digestive juices are secreted into our mouth. Why does this happen?

(a) Because digestive process starts even before you put food in our mouth. So, saliva is secreted

(b) To make solution of solid food we eat

(c) Because it encourages you to put that food into your mouth

(d) It is malfunctioning of our body that saliva secretes into our mouth before we put food in it

19. The statements given below summaries the digestion process in a random order. Arrange them in a sequence and select the correct option.

  I. Removal of faeces.

  II. Food is mixed with saliva.

  III. Churning of food.

  IV. Addition of digestive juices to the food completely.

  V. Absorption of remaining nutrients and water.

Codes

(a) II, III, IV, V and I

(b) II, V, IV, III and I

(c) II, III, V, I and IV

(d) V, IV, III, II and I

Food, Health and Disease

1 Mark Questions

1. Among the food items mentioned below, which one will yield the highest amount of energy after the food is digested
(a) rice
(b) fresh fruits
(c) butter
(d) eggs

2. What do you think should come in the empty boxes, so that this becomes a balanced diet?

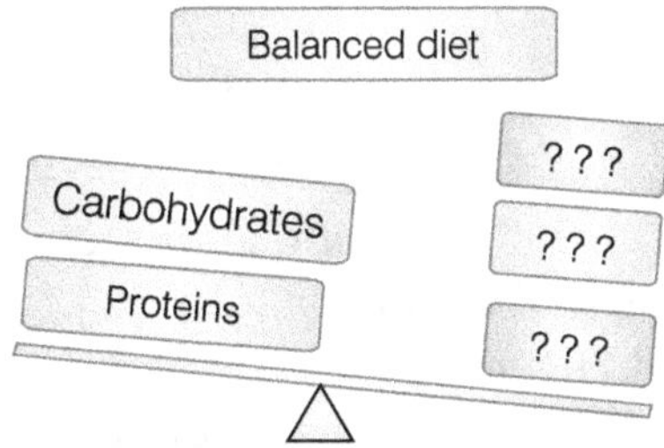

(a) Fat, salt and vitamins
(b) Fats, minerals and vitamins
(c) Sugar, fats and vitamins
(d) Proteins, fats and sugars

3. The two body building foods among the given food items are
(a) oil and ghee
(b) bread and potato
(c) cereals and milk
(d) eggs and meat

4. Bread, potato, sugar, honey are food items that
(a) make us obese
(b) gives us energy
(c) protect us from diseases
(d) prevents constipation

5. Identify the vitamin whose deficiency can cause loss of bone density and increase the risk of fractures in a person.
(a) Vitamin-B   (b) Vitamin-D
(c) Vitamin-A   (d) Vitamin-C

6. By which deficiency disease a person is suffering from, if he is having bleeding gums and swelling of joints?
(a) Typhoid   (b) Scurvy
(c) Malaria   (d) Goitre

7. Arjun fell ill and often develops fever. His medical tests identified a lack of iodine in his body. Doctor advised him to add iodised salt in his meal to avoid the risk of
(a) osteoporosis   (b) anaemia
(c) beri beri   (d) goitre

8. It is an essential part of diet. It remains undigested in the body but helps in digestion of food and removal of waste. What is it?
(a) Proteins   (b) Roughage
(c) Carbohydrates   (d) Water

9. Most cooked food items should be kept in refrigerators. This is because
(a) food gets spoiled faster outside
(b) it occupies lot of space outside
(c) it makes food more healthy
(d) it adds flavour to food

10. It is a communicable disease. It can cause death by damaging the immune system. It is caused by HIV. Which disease is it?
(a) AIDS   (b) Polio
(c) Typhoid   (d) Dengue

11. Mr. Veggy says that vegetarians do not get adequate proteins. Is he correct? Why?
(a) Yes, we get proteins only from chicken and eggs
(b) No, because vegetarian products like milk, cheese, pulses, soya are good sources of proteins
(c) He may be correct
(d) It does not make any difference as proteins are not that much important

12. Match the following components with the role they play and choose the correct option.

	Column I		Column II
A.	Water	1.	Needed in small amounts for proper functioning of body.
B.	Proteins	2.	Removes waste as urine and sweat.
C.	Vitamins	3.	Needed for vision healthy skin, teeth etc.
D.	Minerals	4.	Essential for growth and muscle building.

Codes

	A	B	C	D			A	B	C	D
(a)	1	4	2	3		(b)	3	2	1	4
(c)	2	4	3	1		(d)	2	3	1	4

13. Match the following diseases and their cause.

	Column I		Column II
A.	Nightblindness	1.	Deficiency of vitamin-C
B.	Beri-beri	2.	Deficiency of vitamin-A
C.	Scurvy	3.	Deficiency of vitamin-B_1
D.	Rickets	4.	Deficiency of vitamin-D

Codes

	A	B	C	D			A	B	C	D
(a)	4	2	3	1		(b)	2	3	1	4
(c)	2	4	3	1		(d)	1	3	2	4

14. Ringworm is a communicable disease because it can spread from one person to another through
  I. sneezing in closed spaces.
  II. deficiency of vitamin-B.
  III. birth from an infected mother.
  IV. towels used by infected person.
Codes
(a) I and IV   (b) II and IV
(c) Only IV   (d) All of these

15. Read the following statements and choose the right option. [T] for True and [F] for False.
  I. Proper rest and regular hours of sleep relaxes our muscles.
  II. Proteins provide us with lots of energy to do work.
  III. Sleep gives time to our body for growth and repair.
  IV. Oils and fats just harm our body.
Codes

	I	II	III	IV			I	II	III	IV
(a)	T	F	T	F		(b)	F	F	T	T
(c)	T	T	F	F		(d)	F	T	F	T

2 Marks Questions

16. Refer ot the given Venn diagram and choose the correct option for *P* and *Q*.

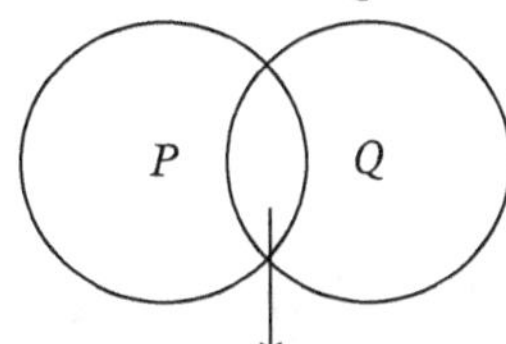

	P	Q
(a)	Fat	Protein
(b)	Carbohydrates	Fats
(c)	Vitamins	Minerals
(d)	Protein	Vitamins

17. Meena was suffering from measles. The doctor told her parents not to send her school for few days. Why do you think doctor stopped her from going to school?

(a) Because measles is a communicable disease and other students can get infected

(b) Because they wanted her to remain with her parents at home

(c) Because measles is a non-communicable disease and can become serious

(d) Because shc will not be able to concentrate on her studies

18. Study the table given below.

Disease	Mode of transmission
Malaria	*A*
B	Direct contact
Cholera	*C*
D	Air

Fill the blanks for labels *A* to *D*.

	A	B	C	D
(a)	Bacteria	Pneumonia	Air	Typhoid
(b)	Virus	Measles	Clothes of infected person	Dengue
(c)	Protozoan	Chickenpox	Contaminated food and water	Flu
(d)	Fungi	Ringworm	Insect bite	Plague

19. Which of the following is not a good eating habit?

(a) Eating uncovered food from roadside

(b) Eating food slowly and chewing it

(c) Brushing teeth twice in a day

(d) Washing hands before and after meals

20. Covid-19 disease is caused by

(a) bacteria

(b) fungi

(c) virus

(d) both (b) and (c)

Water and Its Uses

1 Mark Questions

1. Which of the following figures shown below does not represent natural source of water?

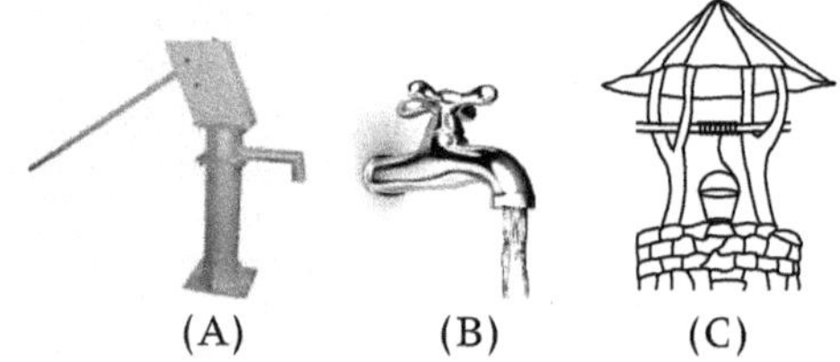

   (a) Only A
   (b) Only B
   (c) Only C
   (d) All of these

2. Rainwater harvesting is
   (a) stopping the water flow to save crops
   (b) providing passage of rainwater to water bodies
   (c) storing underground water
   (d) collecting rainwater and storing it for long term use

3. To test the floating ability of substance in water Varun placed a hollow steel container in water filled tub. The container will
   (a) sink
   (b) float
   (c) first it will sink then float
   (d) first it will float then sink

4. Given below are name of a few process

   > Distillation, sedimentation, filteration, evaporation, decantation, condensation

   How many of these processes can be used to remove soluble impurities from water?
   (a) 3
   (b) 2
   (c) 4
   (d) 6

5. Which of the following impurities can be identified as water insoluble?
   (a) Salt
   (b) Sugar
   (c) Sand
   (d) Alcohol

6. Which process of purifying water can kill the germs that are present in water?
   I. Boiling
   II. Chlorination
   III. Condensation
   IV. Sedimentation
   (a) I and II
   (b) III and IV
   (c) I, II and III
   (d) II, III and IV

7.

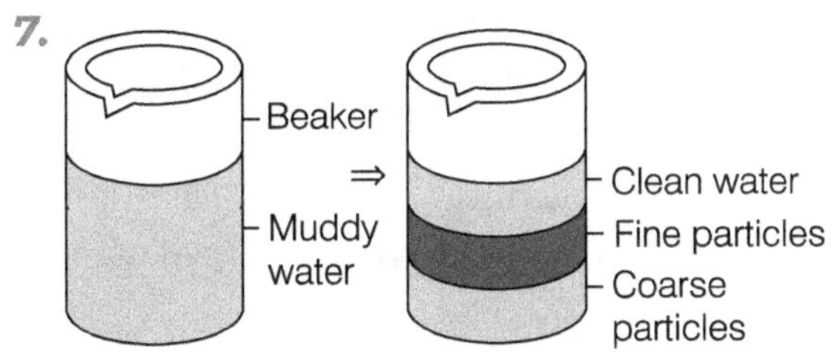

Which process of water purification is shown in the above figure?
(a) Purification   (b) Decantation
(c) Sedimentation   (d) Filtration

8. This year Jaya's village had very low rain fall. The villagers are scared that underground water level will deplete. What is the reason for behind their worries?

   I. Continuous evaporation.

   II. Excessive pumping of ground water.

   III. Groundwater level never changes.

   The correct reason is explained by
   (a) I and II   (b) I and III
   (c) Only III   (d) Only II

9. Choose the odd one out with regard to the floating properties in water.
   (a) Oil   (b) Ice
   (c) Mud   (d) Raisin

10. Match the following columns.

Column I		Column II
A.	Wells	1.	Natural source of water
B.	Glacier	2.	High salt content
C.	Rain	3.	Freshwater body
D.	Ocean	4.	Groundwater

Codes

	A	B	C	D		A	B	C	D
(a)	1	2	3	4	(b)	4	3	1	2
(c)	1	3	4	2	(d)	4	3	2	1

11. Identify the incorrect statements.
   (a) Solubility of water increases with temperature.
   (b) Rain is the purest form of natural water.
   (c) Groundwater is susceptible to contamination by human and animal wastes.
   (d) Filteration can remove very fine impurities from water.

12. Manav took two glasses of water and placed a lemon in each of them. He added salt in glass 1 gradually and left the other glass as such. Which of his observations are correct for what happened next?
   (a) Lemon in glass 2 floated
   (b) Lemon in glass 1 floated
   (c) Both lemon sank
   (d) Lemon in glass 1 sank

13. Alum is added to the sedimentation tank in water treatment plants because
   (a) it can kill the bacteria
   (b) it can speed up sedimentation
   (c) it removes unwanted odours from water
   (d) it can remove finer suspended particles

14. State (T) for True or (F) for False using options given below

   I. Life is possible on Earth even without water.

   II. Evaporation takes place in groundwater also.

   III. Water changes into ice when heated at sufficient temperature.

   IV. Decantation is a process of water purification.

Codes

	I	II	III	IV		I	II	III	IV
(a)	T	F	T	F	(b)	T	F	F	T
(c)	F	T	T	T	(d)	F	T	F	T

15. Choose the incorrect statement.

   I. An object floats on a liquid if its density is less than that of liquid.

   II. An object floats on a liquid if its density is more than that of liquid.

   III. Oil floats on water because its density is less than water.

Codes

(a) Only I   (b) Only II

(c) Only III   (d) All are correct

16. The village panchayat of Raghu's village decided to set up a water purification plant. The main stages of the purifying water in the plant are listed below (not necessarily in sequence).

   I. Filtration   II. Distillation

   III. Sedimentation   IV. Chlorination

   V. Boiling

Which of the following options shows the correct sequence of the stages to be followed?

(a) I → II → III

(b) I → V → IV

(c) II → V → IV

(d) III → II → V

2 Marks Questions

17. On a sunny day, Rohan kept three containers which are shown below having equal amount of water on the terrace. After two hours, he noticed that water in each container is less than the amount of water he kept.

Which of the following container will contain least quantity of water? Which phenomenon is responsible for the loss of water?

(a) I, Evaporation   (b) II, Evaporation

(c) III, Condensation (d) III, Evaporation

18. In cold drinks, we see bubbles forming inside the bottle. Why does this bubble move upwards in a bottle?

(a) Bubbles tends to move upward

(b) Bubbles are made up of lighter gases than cold drink

(c) Due to friction

(d) Due to heating

19. Stuti has prepared four set ups to check the solubility of some solid substances in water. The set up she prepared are shown below.

Her observations are which one of these is correct?
(a) Sugar, salt and chalk powder are soluble in water, but nail fillings are not
(b) Sugar and salt are soluble in water, but chalk powder and nail fillings are insoluble
(c) Salt and chalk powder are soluble, but sugar and nail fillings are insoluble in water
(d) Sugar, salt and chalk powder are insoluble, but nail fillings are soluble in water

20. Raju and Shyam were camping in the wild. They both saw a source of water. But they both decided that they cannot drink water from this source. Which of the following option(s) is/are responsible for their decision.
(a) Water was smelling bad
(b) Water had greenish colour
(c) There were mosquitoes and flies around the water source
(d) All of the above

21. Complete the given passage using suitable words given in options below :
......*A*....... is a technique of collecting and storing rainwater, so that it can be used for various ......*B*...... activities like drinking as well as for ......*C*...... of fields. It helps in ......*D*...... water scarcity in a natural way. Also, it helps in avoiding ......*E*......
depletion.

	A	*B*	*C*	*D*	*E*
(a)	Groundwater	irrigation	domestic	reducing	rainwater harvesting
(b)	Rainwater harvesting	reducing	domestic	irrigation	groundwater
(c)	Groundwater	domestic	irrigation	reducing	rainwater harvesting
(d)	Rainwater harvesting	domestic	irrigation	reducing	groundwater

Matter and Materials

1 Mark Questions

1. Water vapour is which form of ice and during which process, water vapour convert into liquid state?
(a) Gaseous, sublimation
(b) Liquid, melting
(c) Solid, evaporation
(d) Gaseous, condensation

2. During winters, we observe some dew drops over the grasses and leaves in the morning.

What causes the formation of dew drops?
(a) Evaporation of water vapours
(b) Condensation of water vapours
(c) Freezing of water vapours
(d) Melting of water vapours

3. Pick one material from the following which is completely soluble in water.
(a) Chalk powder
(b) Tea leaves
(c) Glucose
(d) Saw dust

4. Two or more substances are combined in an indefinite amount to form
(a) compound   (b) molecule
(c) element   (d) mixture

5. When Ram saw the four objects : Block of wood, air in a balloon, milk in a tetrapack, juice in a glass. Then, he wanted to know which object possess highest force of attraction between particles.

Select the correct option.
(a) Air in balloon
(b) Block of wood
(c) Juice in a glass
(d) Milk in a tetrapack

6. Observe the various arrangements of molecules shown below:

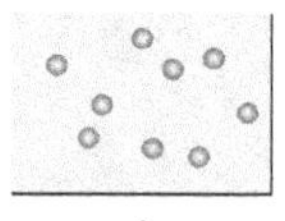 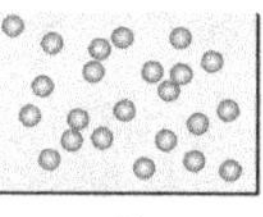 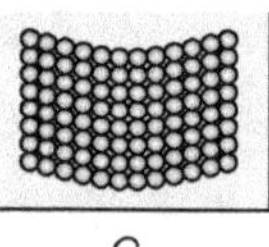

Identify the one option which is wood, oxygen and oil.
Codes

	A	B	C
(a)	Wood	Oil	Oxygen
(b)	Oxygen	Oil	Wood
(c)	Oil	Oxygen	Wood
(d)	Oxygen	Wood	Oil

7. The temperature at which water gets converted into water vapour is known as
   (a) melting
   (b) boiling point
   (c) freezing point
   (d) evaporation point

8. Read the following statements and choose the correct option.
   Statement I Anythings which has mass and occupies space is called matter.
   Statement II Mass is the amount of space, which is occupied by the body.
   (a) Statement I is correct, II is incorrect
   (b) Statement II is correct, I is incorrect
   (c) Both statements are correct
   (d) Both statements are incorrect

9. Which type of material is used for making the front glass (wind screen) of a car?
   (a) Transparent   (b) Translucent
   (c) Opaque   (d) All of these

10. Which of the following statement is true about a compound ?
    (a) They are formed by mixing two or more substances in any proportion
    (b) They are formed by mixing two or more substances in fixed proportion
    (c) Either (a) or (b)
    (d) Neither (a) nor (b)

11. When a substance changes from liquid state to gaseous state, the speed of the particles of the substance
    (a) increases
    (b) decreases
    (c) remains same
    (d) None of the above

12. Which of the following examples listed below constitutes a chemical change?
    (a) Mixing salt and sugar
    (b) Mixing sand and sugar
    (c) Conversion of milk into curd
    (d) Boiling water

13. Brenda took three matters *A*, *B* and *C* of same mass and placed them in three containers of same dimensions as shown below:

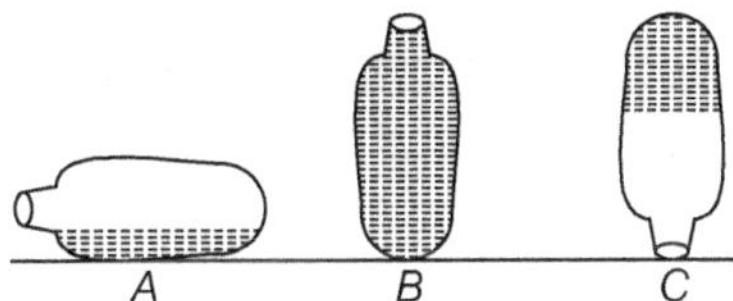

    Which of the following options represent the correct state of matter as per her experiment shown?

	A	B	C
(a)	Liquid	Liquid	Solid
(b)	Solid	Solid	Gas
(c)	Solid	Liquid	Gas
(d)	Liquid	Gas	Solid

2 Marks Questions

Direction (Q.Nos. 14-15) Observe the flow chart given below carefully and answer the questions that follow :

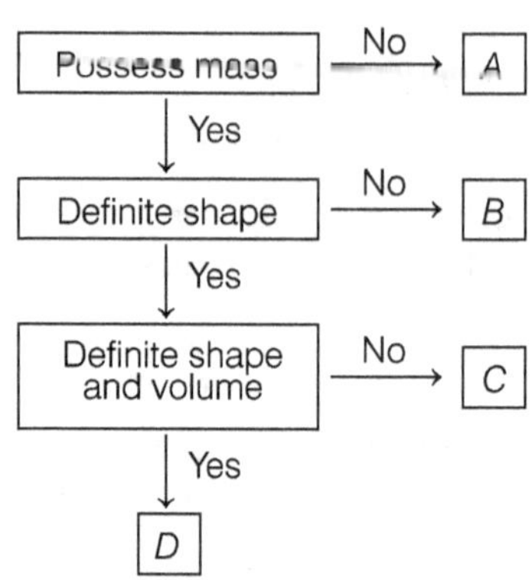

14. Which of the following is likely to be A?

(a) Air   (b) Shadow
(c) Rock   (d) Cold drink

15. Which of the following statements are true about B, C and D?

  I. B is a liquid.

  II. C is a gas.

  III. D is a solid.

  IV. B, C and D are matter.

Codes

(a) Only I   (b) Only II
(c) III and IV   (d) All are correct

16. Observe the following diagram carefully which represents change of state of a substance using some processes A, B, C and D.

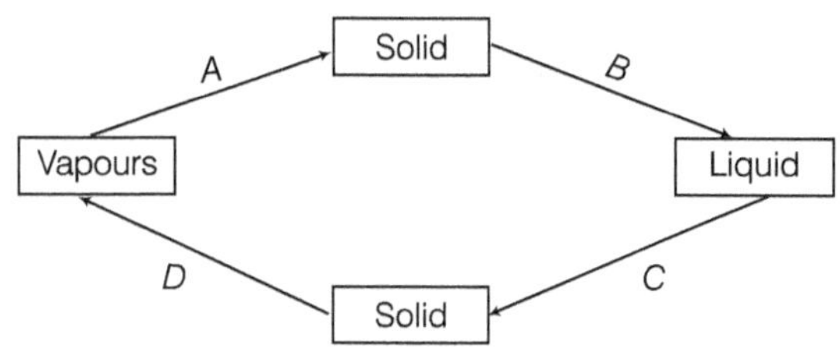

Which of the following options correctly represents A, B, C and D?

	A	B	C	D
(a)	Melting	Condensation	Sublimation	Freezing
(b)	Freezing	Sublimation	Condensation	Melting
(c)	Sublimation	Freezing	Melting	Condensation
(d)	Condensation	Melting	Freezing	Sublimation

17. Observe the flow chart shown below carefully.

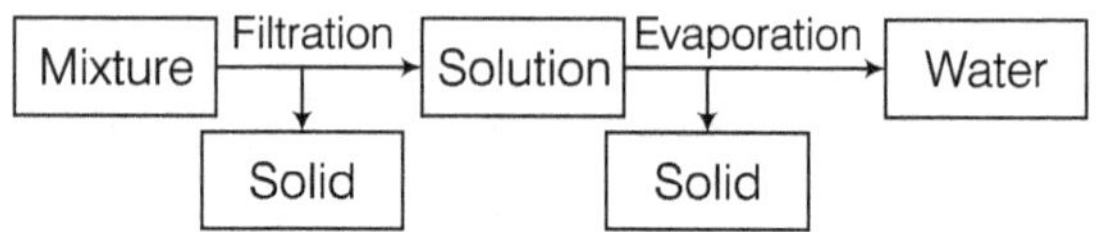

Which of the following options depicts the mixture correctly ?

(a) Sand + Oil + Water
(b) Carbon dioxide + Salt + Water
(c) Stones + Rice + Water
(d) Sand + Salt + Water

18. A student dissolves sugar into pure water. Which among the following statement is correct?

(a) The student will observe an increase in the weight of water
(b) The student will observe an increase in the density of water
(c) The student will observe the water becomes translucent
(d) The student will observe the water becomes opaque

19. Based on the given experiment done by students. They make some statements on change in state of water

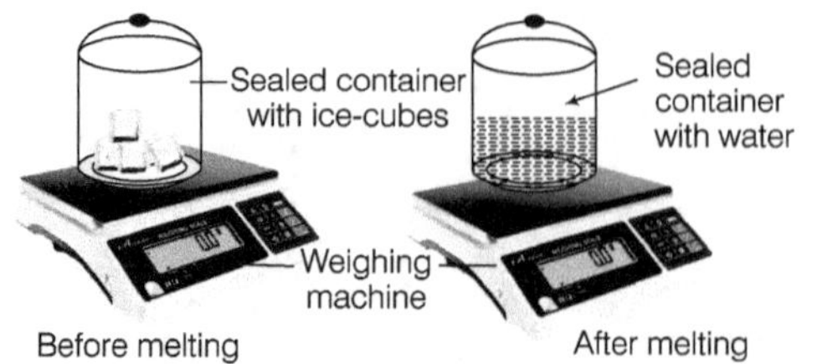

Rohit The mass of container having water will be less than the mass of the container having ice-cubes.

Charlie The mass of container having water will be same as the mass of container having ice-cubes.

Sumit The mass of container having water will be more than the mass of container having ice cubes.

Who gave the correct statement?
(a) Rohit　　　　(b) Sumit
(c) Charlie　　　(d) Either (a) or (b)

20. State true (T) or false (F) using options given below.

I. The capacity of a liquid to have definite volume enables it to change its shape as per the container.

II. Mass is the measure of how much material is contained in a matter.

III. Gases do not possess any mass and volume.

IV. Mixture contains definite proportion of two or more elements.

V. Any massless particle that occupies space is considered to be matter.

Codes

	I	II	III	IV	V
(a)	F	F	F	F	T
(b)	T	T	T	T	F
(c)	F	T	F	F	F
(d)	T	T	F	F	F

Work, Force and Energy

1 Mark Questions

1. Two boys A and B are applying a force on the door as shown below:

   Which of them applies push force and pull force?

	Push	Pull
(a)	B	A
(b)	A	B
(c)	A	A
(d)	B	B

2. Rohan carries three blocks A, B and C wrapped in gift paper. In order to check which substance is aluminium, he brought each one of them near a magnet as shown below and recorded the observation.

Object	Observation
A	It moved towards the magnet.
B	It did not move.
C	It moved away from the magnet.

   Which of them is aluminium?
   (a) A
   (b) B
   (c) C
   (d) Both (a) and (c)

3. Which of the following is a characteristic of simple machine?
   (a) They are not very large
   (b) They have few or no moving parts
   (c) They take a long time to make
   (d) They run on electricity

4. An inclined plane and a screw is shown in the figure below:

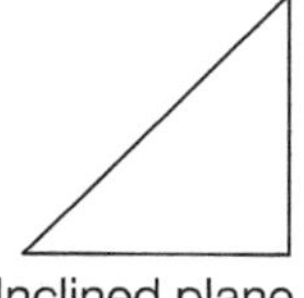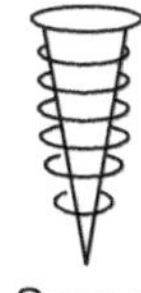

   Which of the following statement(s) is/are true in context with the figures?

   I. An inclined plane is a screw.

   II. A screw is an inclined plane.

   III. Both inclined plane and screw are two different simple machines.

   Codes
   (a) Only I
   (b) Only II
   (c) Only III
   (d) Either I or II

5. Observe the diagram shown below carefully which depicts a wedge being used to cut a log of wood.

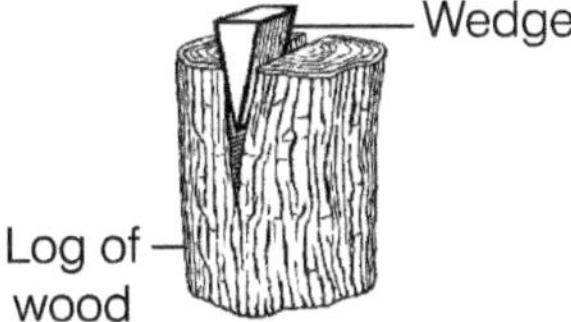

Which of the following options correctly shows the direction of force exerted on wedge and force acting on the wood?

	Force exerted on wedge	Force exerted on the wood
(a)	↑	←→
(b)	↓	←←
(c)	↑	→←
(d)	↓	←→

6. Choose the incorrect option.
(a) Car tyre–Road–Friction force
(b) Iron–Magnet–Magnetic force
(c) Floating boats–Buoyant force
(d) Ships–Spring force

7. What is the force that stops us from slipping when we walk?
(a) Gravity   (b) Friction
(c) Air resistance   (d) Upthrust

8. Ryan and Romeo are playing with a ball. They both are standing at a distance and facing each other. Ryan throws the ball towards Romeo and Romeo catches the ball and throws it again towards Ryan. The game goes on in this manner. Which of the following conclusion can be made from this activity?
(a) Both of them applies force to throw the ball
(b) The direction of motion of the ball changes when Ryan applies force to it

(c) Romeo applies force to stop the ball. The ball slows down because of the force applied by Romeo
(d) All of the above

9. While carrying an electric iron, Selvi accidently drops it on the floor because of which a small crack was formed on the floor. Which force was acting on the iron during this incident?
(a) Muscular force   (b) Electric force
(c) Reaction force   (d) Friction force

10. The figure given below shows few children playing the game of tug of war.

While initiating the game, the knot on the rope did not shift at first. Why is it so?
(a) Both teams had the same total mass
(b) One team applied a greater force than the other team
(c) Both teams applied an equal force in the same direction on the rope
(d) Both teams applied an equal force in opposite directions on the rope

11. The figure below shows a well. Which type of simple machine is used in the given figure?

(a) Pulley
(b) Wheel and axle
(c) Lever
(d) Both (a) and (b)

12. Rohit and his friends are playing basketball which is shown below.

When Rohit throws the basketball in the upward direction, it reaches to a maximum height and then falls back. What happens to its kinetic energy at the highest point?
(a) It becomes maximum
(b) It becomes half
(c) It becomes zero
(d) Ball does not have any kind of energy

13. The diagram given below shows a ball sliding down a slope.

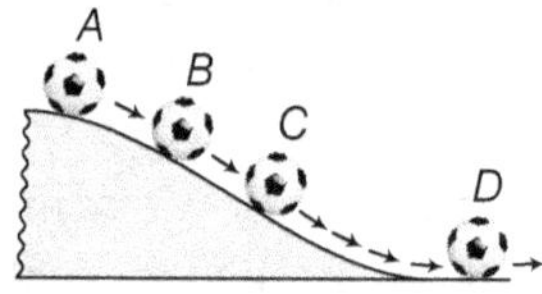

At which position, the ball will possess maximum potential energy and kinetic energy, respectively?
(a) A and B
(b) C and B
(c) D and A
(d) A and D

14. A boy is playing with a toy car which is shown below.

The energy changes that make the car move are
(a) electrical energy $\rightarrow$ kinetic energy
(b) chemical energy $\rightarrow$ electrical energy
(c) chemical energy $\rightarrow$ electrical energy $\rightarrow$ kinetic energy
(d) None of the above

2 Marks Questions

15. Column I represents simple machine and Column II represents the use of the simple machine. Match the Column I with Column II and choose the correct option.

	Column I		Column II
A.	Axle	1.	Flyovers
B.	Pulley	2.	Nail cutters
C.	Inclined plane	3.	Car tyres
D.	Lever	4.	Axe
E.	Wedge	5.	Elevators

Codes

	A	B	C	D	E
(a)	5	4	2	3	1
(b)	1	2	3	5	4
(c)	3	5	1	2	4
(d)	1	5	4	2	3

16. Observe the figure of a stapler as shown below.

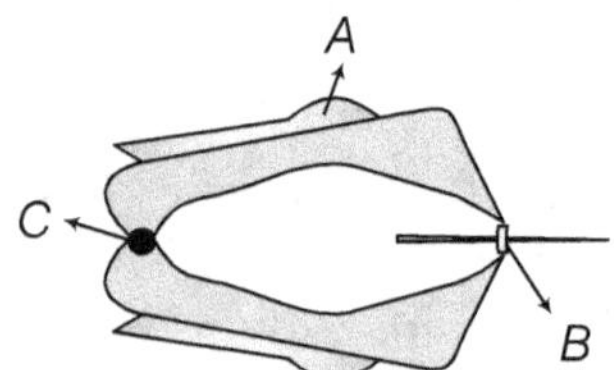

Choose the option which correctly labels the parts marked as *A*, *B* and *C*.

	A	*B*	*C*
(a)	Load	Fulcrum	Effort
(b)	Effort	Load	Fulcrum
(c)	Fulcrum	Load	Effort
(d)	Effort	Fulcrum	Load

17. An athlete throws a javelin which is shown in the figure given below. The javelin stays in the mid-air at point *X* before landing to the ground.

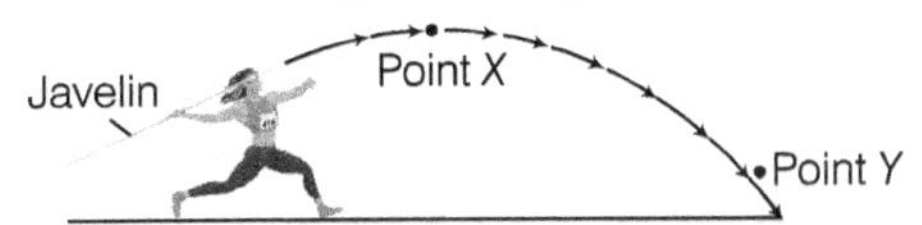

Which of the following statement is true regarding the motion of javelin?
(a) No force is acting on the javelin when it is at point *X*
(b) The javelin travels at the same speed from point *X* to point *Y*
(c) Gravitational force only acts on the javelin when it is at point *X*
(d) Gravitational force is acting on the javelin from point *X* to point *Y*

18. Observe the figures shown below in which Raghu is trying to pull two boxes filled with different substances.

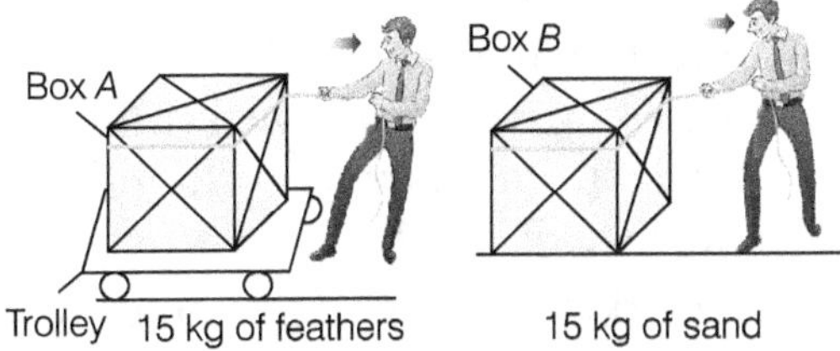

It was difficult for him to pull box *B* as compared to that of box *A*.
Which of the following explain the reason correctly?
  I. Less force is required to pull box *A*.
 II. The sand is heavier than the feathers.

III. There is no friction between box *B* and the floor.
Codes
(a) Only I   (b) Both II and III
(c) Both I and III   (d) All are correct

19. Sam made two set ups in order to observe the magnetic force which is shown below.

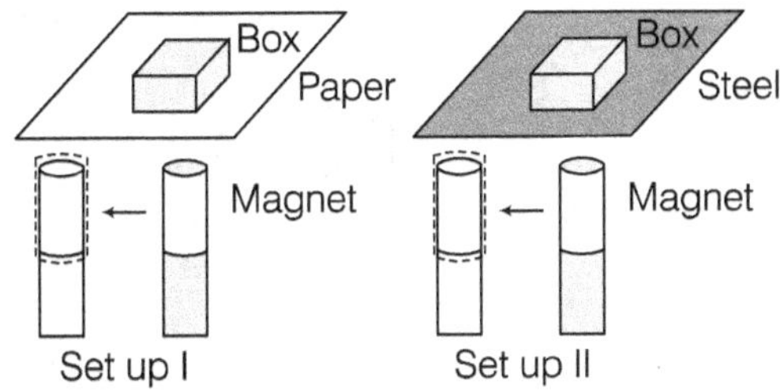

When he moves the magnets in both the set ups, in which case the box will move?
(a) Set up I
(b) Set up II
(c) Both (a) and (b)
(d) Neither (a) nor (b)

20. Solve the crossword and answer the following questions.

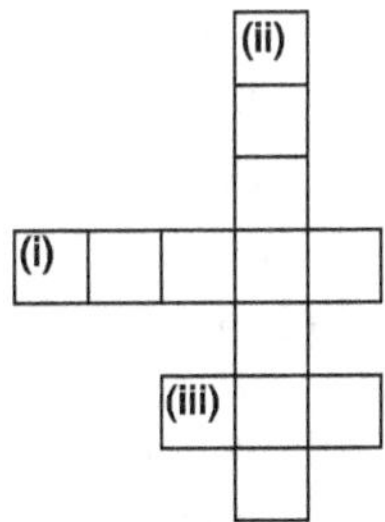

(i) Hydroelectric power makes electricity by using energy from falling.
(a) Winds (b) Water (c) Tides (d) Waves
(ii) In running, you have this kind of energy.
(a) Potential   (b) Kinetic
(c) Gravity   (d) Thermal
(iii) All machines used for transportation use this fossil fuel.
(a) Coal   (b) Wax   (c) Oil   (d) Gas

Environment and Natural Calamities

1 Mark Questions

1. Everything surrounding us and affecting us is called environment. Choose the biotic components of the environment from the given options.
   (a) Animals and soil
   (b) Air and water
   (c) Animals and plants
   (d) Water and sunlight

2. X is a gas used in refrigerators, air conditioners in aeroplanes and jets. However its release in the environment has many adverse effects. Identify X
   (a) Carbon dioxide
   (b) Methane
   (c) Carbon monoxide
   (d) Chlorofluorocarbons

3. What do you think was the reason behind Taj Mahal turning yellow?
   (a) Harmful gases released from the factories near it
   (b) Due to white marble getting old
   (c) It was actually yellow marble polished white and now white colour has been washed away
   (d) Due to too many tourists visiting the place

4. Which of the following have adverse effects on the environment?
   (a) Burning of dead leaves
   (b) Use of fossil fuels
   (c) Excessive used of AC and refrigerators
   (d) All of the above

5. Identify the pair of materials which will not cause soil pollution?
   (a) Fruit peel and paper bag
   (b) Ceramic mug and polythene bag
   (c) Pen and pencils
   (d) Jute bags and plastic toys

6. Earthquakes are caused by severe shock waves that travel through solid rocks from below the ground to the surface of Earth.

   The point below the ground, where an earthquake begins is called as
   (a) epicentre (b) focus
   (c) richter scale (d) core

7. A volcano's that has not erupted in the last 10,000 years but cannot be confirmed as dead is
   (a) Mt Etna (b) Mt Kilimanjaro
   (c) Mt Fuji (d) None of these

8. An erupting volcano can trigger, how many of the other calamities mentioned below :

Cyclones, tsunami, drought, earthquakes, forest fires, storms, rock falls, floods.

(a) 5   (b) 7   (c) 3   (d) 4

9. Complete the analogy

Tsunami : ...... :: Earthquakes : Land
(a) Water
(b) Air
(c) Underground
(d) None of the above

10. Match the following columns.

	Column I		Column II
A.	Extinct volcano	1.	Strong, fast spinning winds
B.	Epicentre	2.	Carbon dioxide, methane and water vapours
C.	Cyclone	3.	The point above focus on earth's surface
D.	Green house gases	4.	Mt Kilimanjaro

Codes

	A	B	C	D			A	B	C	D
(a)	4	1	2	3		(b)	3	2	1	4
(c)	4	3	1	2		(d)	1	4	2	3

11. We all know that global warming results in increased temperature of the Earth's surface.

This phenomenon is considered an adverse effect of air pollution because

   I. It will cause melting of ice caps.

  II. It will decrease the level of water in oceans.

Which of the two given statement is correct?
Codes
(a) Statement I is correct
(b) Statement II is correct
(c) Both statements are correct
(d) Both statements are incorrect

12. Excess nitrate (a fertiliser) is a very common pollutant in rivers, which causes rapid growth of algae and death of aquatic plants present at the bottom. The lack of which of the following factor is responsible for the death of these aquatic plants?
(a) Carbon dioxide
(b) Oxygen and carbon dioxide
(c) Light and oxygen
(d) Nitrogen

13. Select the incorrect statement.

   I. Use of plastic bags should be reduced.

  II. Garbage should be thrown at proper dumping places.

 III. Wastes are to be dumped directly into water bodies.

 IV. Tall chimneys are used with filters to let out smoke and gases.
Codes
(a) Only I
(b) Only II
(c) Only III
(d) Only IV

2 Marks Questions

14. Read the given statements and choose the correct option.

Statement I The rate of melting of glaciers and mountains ice caps are increasing due to global warming.

Statement II The effects of global warming are reversible and can be controlled rapidly.

Codes
(a) Statement I is correct
(b) Statement II is correct
(c) Both statement I are correct
(d) Both statements are incorrect

15. One hot summer day, Veer planned to go out with his family in his car which was parked outside in the Sun. When they opened and sat in the car, they found it to be extremely hot even more than the outside, because
(a) AC of the car was not working
(b) Car became a greenhouse
(c) As the car was closed, so there was no cool air inside the car
(d) Car is made up of metal, so it became hot

16. Ravi classified some common wastes into two categories and wrote his observations about them.

Category I	Category II
Paper towels	Pepsi can
Grasses, weeds dried leaves	Bisleris empty bottle
Fruit and vegetable peels	Aluminium foil

Which one of his observation are correct?
(a) All materials in I are non-biodegradable.
(b) Category II materials take a short time to degrade.
(c) Category I things remain in environment forever.
(d) Cateogry II materials pollute the environment and should be recycled.

17. Read the statements given below and select the option that correctly states them as true (T) and false (F).
  I. Earthquake with an intensity of 7-8 richter causes no serious damage.
  II. Volcanic eruptions causes air pollution
  III. Damage to ozone layer is caused by carbon dioxide.
  IV. Drinking contaminated water can cause malaria.

Codes

	I	II	III	IV		I	II	III	IV
(a)	T	F	T	F	(b)	F	T	F	F
(c)	T	F	F	T	(d)	F	F	T	T

18. Disaster management institute conducted a workshop for schools on Do's and Don'ts during natural disasters. Children were asked to run away from a particular natural disaster in a mock drill. Based on the picture, the disaster can identified as

(a) Cyclone
(b) Earthquake
(c) Tsunami
(d) Volcanic eruption

Natural Resources

1 Mark Questions

1. Air is a mixture of gases as shown in the figure given below

   Which component is used by human beings and other animals to survive?

   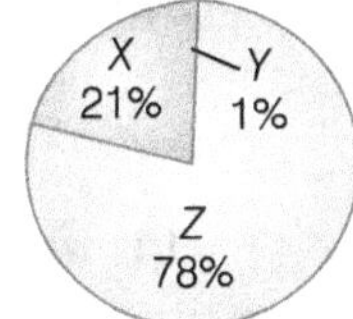

   (a) X (b) Y
   (c) Z (d) Both X and Y

2. Our atmosphere is a protective blanket formed around the Earth.

   Which layer helps in preventing the entry of harmful UV rays on the Earth?
   (a) Exosphere
   (b) Thermosphere and mesosphere
   (c) Stratosphere
   (d) Troposphere

3. Refer to the figure given below

   What happens when we place an empty glass over the candle?

   (a) It will keep burning
   (b) It will stop burning
   (c) It will burn slowly
   (d) Both (a) and (c)

4. Aditya prepared three pots A, B and C for planting new saplings. He filled pot A with sand, Pot B with loam and C with clayey soil. He watered them regularly and recorded his observation.

   Which of his pot (A, B and C) will successfully grow into new plant?
   (a) Pot C
   (b) Pot A
   (c) Pot B
   (d) Both A and C

5. It is a six letters metamorphic rock made up of limestone and it is found in many colours.
   (a) Basalt   (b) Marble
   (c) Gneiss   (d) Pumice

6. Read the statements given below and identify the one that is incorrect.
   (a) Limestone is a sedimentary rock
   (b) Sandstone is used as a body scrubber
   (c) Fossils are found beneath sedimentary rocks
   (d) Petroleum is also called black gold

7. Which of the following shows a result of deforestation and the effect it has on the environment.

	Result	Effect
(a)	Fewer flowering plants	Reduced CO_2 in air
(b)	Fewer trees	Increased humidity of air
(c)	More ground cover	Wind removes soil
(d)	More water flows away	Soil washed away

8. Match the different types of rocks with their way of formation.

A.	Sedimentary rocks	1.	Granite
B.	Igneous rocks	2.	Shale
C.	Metamorphic rocks	3.	Quartzite

Codes

	A	B	C			A	B	C
(a)	1	2	3		(b)	3	1	2
(c)	2	1	3		(d)	1	3	2

9. Two balloons of equal size were filled with air and tied at the opposite ends of a beam balance. One of the balloons is pricked to let air escape from it. We observe that the side of beam balance with the air filled balloon tilts downward.

Four students have made their observation with respect to the above experiment.

Student I. Air occupies space

Student II. Air has weight

Student III. Air exerts pressure

Student IV. Air is a mixture of gases

Which student observation(s) is/are correct?
(a) I and II
(b) Only II
(c) II and IV
(d) Only III

10. Ramu, son of a farmer noticed that in between two crops his father used to grow some cover crops like grass, pea, etc. Why his father does so?
(a) To keep himself busy in the free time between two crops
(b) Roots of cover crops hold the soil particles together and prevent them from erosion
(c) He had excess of seeds so he's just using them
(d) To earn extra money

11. The process X helps in soil formation whereas Y contributes to erosion of soil. Identify processes X and Y and select the correct option regarding them.
(a) Processes X and Y are dependent on the water
(b) X could be weathering whereas Y could be deforestation
(c) X could be overgrazing whereas Y could be afforestation
(d) X and Y are man made activities

12. Identify the type of rock from the two statement given below
  I. Rock X is a sedimentary rock.
  II. It is formed from shells and skeletons of small sea creatures.
Choose the correct option.
(a) Limestone
(b) Conglomerate
(c) Sandstone
(d) Shale

13. Fossil fuels are formed from remains of plant and animals. We need to conserve them because,

   I. they are expensive.

  II. they are not much in India, we have to import them.

 III. they take millions of years to form.

 IV. they release harmful gases and cause pollution.

Codes

(a) III and IV   (b) I and II
(c) I and III   (d) II and IV

14. Refer to the figure given below

Which of the following statement is correct regarding it?

15. State True [T] or False [F] using options given below.

I. It is a method of reducing soil erosion by wind.

II. It is practised only in mountainous regions.

III. It represents embankments.

Codes

(a) I and II   (b) All of these
(c) Only II   (d) None of these

15. State True [T] or False [F] using options given below.

   I. Flooded rivers and running waters remove the top soil.

  II. There is no human factor responsible for soil erosion.

 III. As a result of soil erosion, the land gains its fertility.

 IV. Strong winds in desert areas blow away lots of topsoil.

Codes

	I	II	III	IV			I	II	III	IV
(a)	T	T	F	F		(b)	T	F	T	F
(c)	F	F	T	T		(d)	T	F	F	T

2 Marks Questions

16. Refer to the flow chart given below and identify the components of air labelled A, B and C.

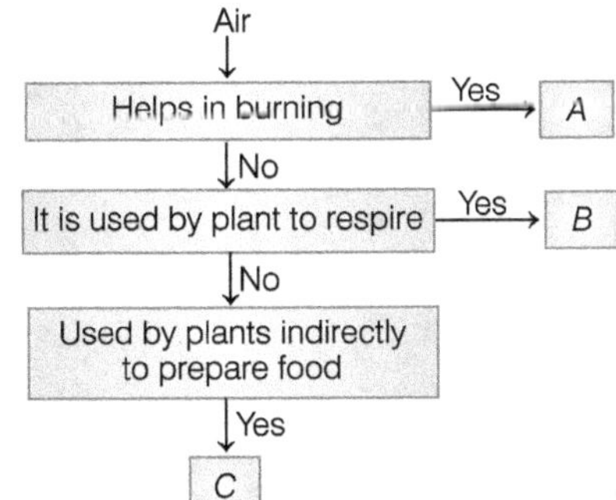

Codes

	A	B	C
(a)	Oxygen	Carbon dioxide	Nitrogen
(b)	Carbon dioxide	Oxygen	Nitrogen
(c)	Nitrogen	Oxygen	Carbon dioxide
(d)	Oxygen	Nitrogen	Carbon dioxide

17. Leena took two pots. In both she put soil and labelled them A and B. In pot A, she planted some small plants, whereas in pot B she placed no plants.

Now after 4-5 days, she pours lots of water in both *A* and *B* with some speed. Which of the two pot *A* or pot *B* will lose more soil?

(a) Pot *A*
(b) Pot *B*
(c) Both will lose soil, equally
(d) None of them will lose any soil

18. Complete the following flow chart which depicts characteristics of rocks and minerals.

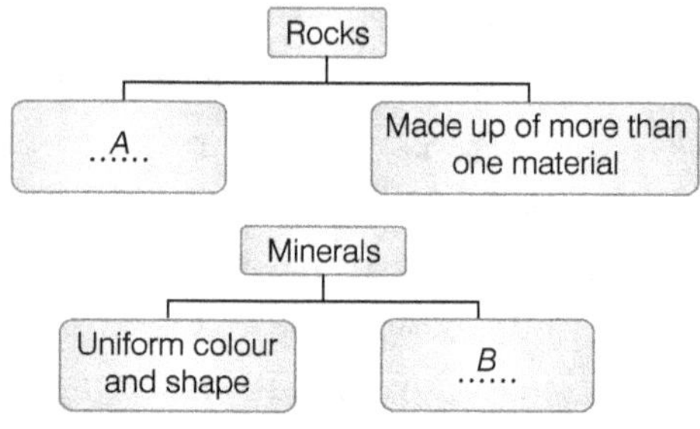

	A	B
(a)	They are different in shape but uniform in colour.	Made up of several substances in different composition
(b)	They are different in shape and colour.	They are pure and have fixed compositions
(c)	They are uniform in shape and colour.	They are made up of more than two substances
(d)	They are different in colour but uniform in shape	Made up of two substances

19. Arrange the sequence of formation of coal in correct order.

  I. Heat and pressure of Earth changed them to hard rock.

  II. Remains of plants on soil.

  III. Matter changed to soft rock.

  IV. Matter got covered with mud and stone.

Codes
(a) I, II, III and IV
(b) IV, III, II and I
(c) II, IV, III and I
(d) II, I, III and IV

20. Read the following statements and choose the correct option.

Statement I Chalk is a kind of limestone.

Statement II Quartzite is formed from sandstone.

Statement III Slate is a form of igneous rock.

(a) All statements are correct
(b) Statement I is incorrect, statements II and III are correct
(c) Statement II is incorrect, statements I and III are correct
(d) Statement III is incorrect, statements II and I are correct

Our Universe

1 Mark Questions

1. Group of stars joined to form patterns in the sky are called
(a) satellite
(b) constellation
(c) celestial
(d) planets

2. The innermost layer of Earth is called… .
(a) crust
(b) mantal
(c) ore
(d) core

3. Why we cannot see stars and Moon during day time?
(a) They are very far from Earth
(b) The Sun is too bright during the day cause them to be less visible.
(c) They do not produce light during day.
(d) Both (b) and (c)

4. The movement of the Earth at its fixed axis is known as rotation. These rotations are responsible for
(a) change in seasons
(b) change in dates of calendar
(c) change in day and night
(d) All of the above

5. Match the following columns.

	Column I		Column II
A.	Pluto	1.	Brightest planet
B.	Mars	2.	Largest planet
C.	Jupiter	3.	Red planet
D.	Venus	4.	Blue planet
E.	Earth	5.	Dwarf planet

Codes

	A	B	C	D	E
(a)	5	3	2	1	4
(b)	3	5	2	1	4
(c)	5	3	1	2	4
(d)	4	3	2	1	5

6. Which of the following is not true about Moon?
(a) It do not emit its own light
(b) It revolve around the Earth
(c) It is a natural satellite
(d) It is the nearest star to Earth

7. Choose the option which on unscrambling gives the name of constellation.
(a) USMARAJOR   (b) ONOIR
(c) PIICOESSAA   (d) All of these

8. Identify X and Y. One is done for you.

Shani : Saturn :: X : Uranus :: Y : Neptune

Choose the correct option.

(a) X - Mangal, Y - Shukra

(b) X - Arun, Y - Budh

(c) X - Brihaspati , Y - Shukra

(d) X - Arun, Y - Varun

9. Consider the diagram shown below which depicts an eclipse.

Which type of eclipse is shown in the above figure?

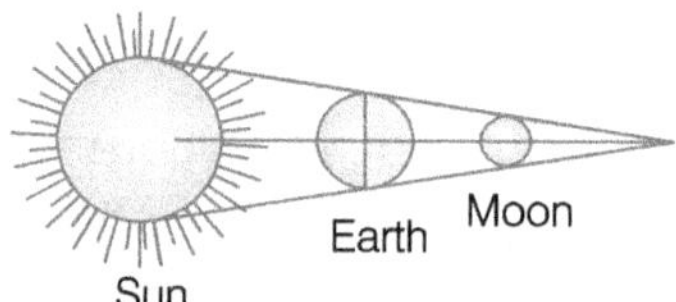

(a) Solar eclipse   (b) Eclipse

(c) Lunar eclipse   (d) Either (a) or (c)

10. The dotted particles in the figure shown below are the asteroids which are found between planet X and planet Y. Identify the planets, respectively.

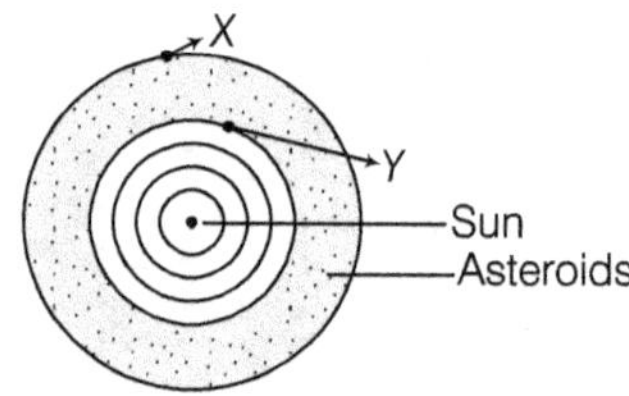

(a) X-Earth, Y-Mars (b) X-Mars, Y-Jupiter

(c) X-Jupiter, Y-Mars (d) X-Saturn, Y-Mars

11. It is mandatory to carry oxygen in gas cylinders to travel into space. Why?

(a) Gas cylinders increase the weight of the body which stabilises the motion of the traveller

(b) Space is lack in oxygen. So, gas cylinders are used for breathing

(c) Oxygen of the gas cylinders provides the direction in space

(d) Both (a) and (b)

12. Observe the diagram shown below carefully which depicts a solar eclipse.

Which of the options best define the position of Earth, Moon and Sun?

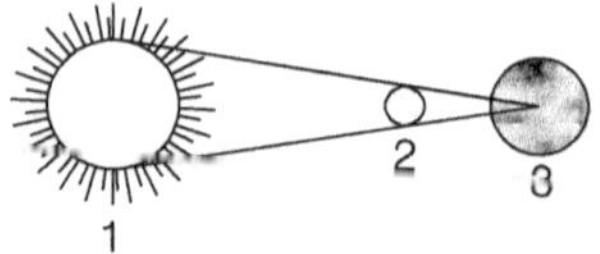

	Earth	Moon	Sun		Earth	Moon	Sun
(a)	1	2	3	(b)	3	2	1
(c)	3	1	2	(d)	2	1	3

13. State true (T) or false (F) using options given below.

I. The rotation of Earth causes two low tides everyday.

II. In the areas between the two high tides, the water forms high tides.

III. The intensity of the tides does not vary with the phases of the Moon.

Codes

	I	II	III		I	II	III
(a)	T	T	F	(b)	T	F	F
(c)	F	F	T	(d)	F	T	T

14. .... was the first Indian satellite launched in ....

(a) Sputnik I, 1957

(b) Aryabhatta, 1959

(c) Aryabhatta, 1975

(d) Sputnik I, 1973

15. Solve the riddle,

(a) Jupiter   (b) Uranus

(c) Saturn   (d) Neptune

2 Marks Questions

16. Consider the following statements about a planet.

   I. Planets revolve around the Sun throughout the year.

   II. Planets shine brightly by the sunlight reflected by them.

Choose the correct statement(s).
(a) Only I is correct
(b) Only II is correct
(c) Both I and II are correct
(d) None of the above

17. Column I represents the objects in the solar system and Column II represents special feature about them. Match the Column I and Column II and choose the correct option.

Column I	Column II
A. Sun	1. Rocky objects revolving around the Sun
B. Saturn	2. Brightest planet
C. Asteroid	3. Dwarf planet
D. Venus	4. Source of energy
E. Pluto	5. Beautiful planet

Codes

	A	B	C	D	E		A	B	C	D	E
(a)	1	2	4	5	3	(b)	3	4	2	5	1
(c)	4	5	1	2	3	(d)	5	1	2	3	4

18. Refer to diagram given below. Identify P and Q.

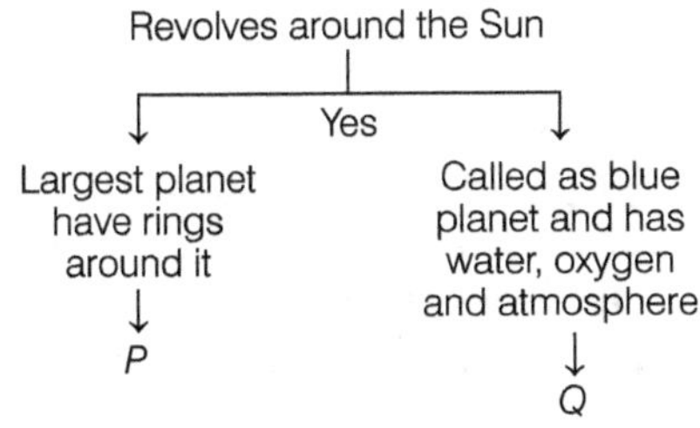

(a) P–Saturn, Q–Uranus
(b) P–Jupiter, Q–Venus
(c) P–Uranus, Q–Earth
(d) P–Jupiter, Q–Earth

19. Refer to the flow chart, identify P, Q, R from the option given below.

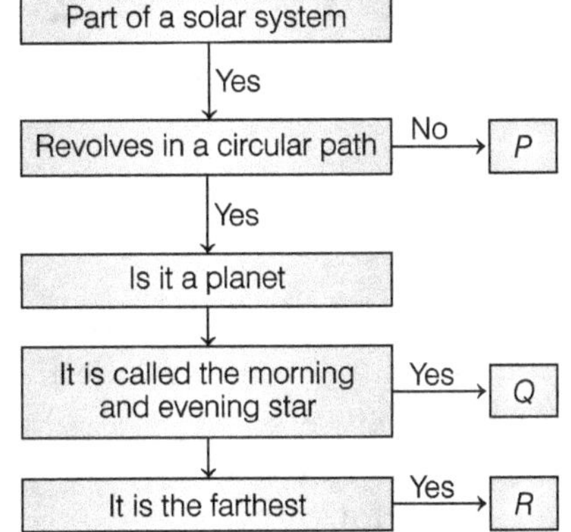

(a) P–Moon, Q–Sun, R–Uranus
(b) P–Sun, Q–Star, R–Pluto
(c) P–Sun, Q–Venus, R–Neptune
(d) P–Pluto, Q–Earth, R–Neptune

20. Students of class 5th made some statements about two planets who made the incorrect statement?

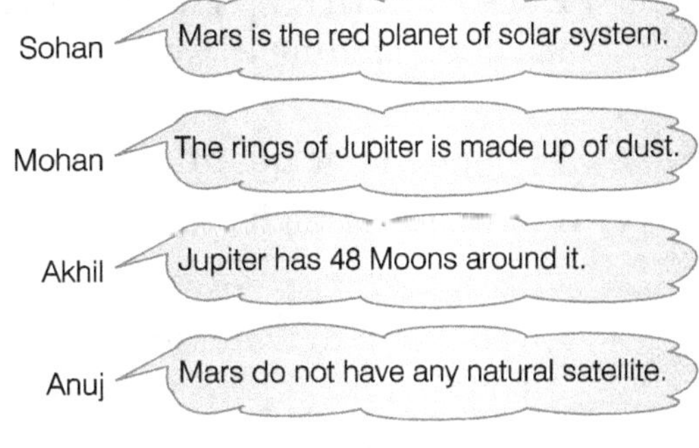

(a) Sohan and Akhil
(b) Mohan and Anuj
(c) Mohan and Akhil
(d) Akhil and Anuj

Farming and Agriculture

1 Mark Questions

1. The practice of production of crop plants at large scale is called
   (a) Horticulture
   (b) Animal husbandry
   (c) Agriculture
   (d) Plant breeding

2. My name is a five letter word. My common name is "corn". I'm a summer season crop. I grow well in dry soil of plains and hills. Who am I?
   (a) Wheat   (b) Maize
   (c) Gourd   (d) Bajra

3. Rice is a Kharif crop grown during the period of June to October. This is because they
   I. require large quantity of water.
   II. require less light.
   III. need low temperature.
   IV. can adapt to water logging conditions.
   Choose the correct option.
   (a) II and IV
   (b) I and III
   (c) Only IV
   (d) All of the above

4. The figure given below represent one of the stages of agricultural process

   (a) enrichment of soil with nutrients
   (b) killing weeds
   (c) loosening the soil
   (d) sowing the seeds

5. Groundnut, fennel, soybean, jawar, cotton and chilly. What is common for all these crops?
   (a) They are Rabi crops
   (b) These crops are harvested in spring season
   (c) These crops are sown during November-April
   (d) They are Kharif crops

6. Which step is incorrectly matched?
   (a) Ploughing–making soil loosened
   (b) Irrigation–sowing seed
   (c) Protection of crop–adding pesticides and insecticides
   (d) Harvesting–cutting down of matured crop

7. Transplanting or replanting is the technique of moving a plant from one location to another.

What is the advantage of transplanting?
(a) It helps the farmers to select only the healthy sapling
(b) Saplings can be planted at a proper distance
(c) It increases the crop production
(d) All of the above

8. Which of the following statement is not true?
(a) Potato is a Rabi crop
(b) Superphosphate helps to enrich the soil in nutrients
(c) Jute is a fibre crop
(d) Seeds should be sown very deep in soil

9. Identify the statement which correctly explains the figure given below.

(a) Manual weeding from the field
(b) Threshing of matured crops
(c) Cutting down the mature crops
(d) Spraying pesticides on the plants

10. Which one of the following statement is not true for insecticides and pesticides?
(a) Both of them should be used on standing crops
(b) Both are chemicals
(c) Both protect the crops from insects
(d) Both should be used in high concentration on the crops

11. Ram's father is a farmer. While storing a drum of rice grains, he added a few dry neem leaves in it. This is for
(a) preventing the grains for spoiling
(b) keeping the birds away
(c) prevent insects from eating the grains
(d) keeping the mice away from grains

12. Refer to the figure given below and answer the following question. Which of the following statement is correctly explaining either process *A* and *B*.

(a) Process *A* is winnowing which separates grain from stalks
(b) Process *B* is threshing which separates the chaff
(c) Process *A* is threshing which separates grain from stalks
(d) Process *B* is harvesting of crops

13. Match Column I with Column II and select the correct option.

	Column I		Column II
A.	Wheat, rice, maize, etc.	1.	Plantation crops
B.	Mustard, sunflower, etc.	2.	Food grain crops
C.	Tea, coffee etc.	3.	Fibre crops
D.	Cotton	4.	Oil rich crops

Codes

	A	B	C	D
(a)	1	2	3	4
(b)	2	4	1	3
(c)	3	2	4	1
(d)	4	1	2	3

14. The steps of agricultural process is given below in a random sequence.

 I. Manuring

 II. Winnowing

 III. Sowing

 IV. Harvesting

 V. Ploughing

Arrange them in the order they are carried out in an agricultural field and select the correct option.

(a) V, I, III, IV and II
(b) I, V, III, II and IV
(c) I, III, V, II and IV
(d) V, II, I, III and IV

15. Most Indian farmers cultivate pulses like arhar, mung, etc., after planting and harvesting cereal crops. Select the most appropriate reason for this practice.

 I. Pulses are legumes.

 II. They can withstand high temperature and humidity and grow healthy.

 III. Pulses can restore the deficiency of nutrients in soil.

Codes

(a) I and III
(b) II and III
(c) I and II
(d) I, II and III

2 Marks Questions

16. Crops are needed to be protected against

 I. Grazing animals like cows and goats.

 II. Air, water and warmth.

 III. Pests like locust, grasshopper.

 IV. Diseases

Codes

(a) Only II
(b) I, II and IV
(c) I, III and IV
(d) II and IV

17. Anita's class went to a farm on a trip to learn more about agriculture. She observed that farmers were removing small plants that are growing across the entire field, surrounding the main crops.

The most reasonable explanation for this process is to

(a) prevent crops from dying
(b) prevent overcrowding of plants on the field
(c) keep a check on infections caused by pests or insects
(d) prepare soil for more main crops.

18. Complete the following structures.

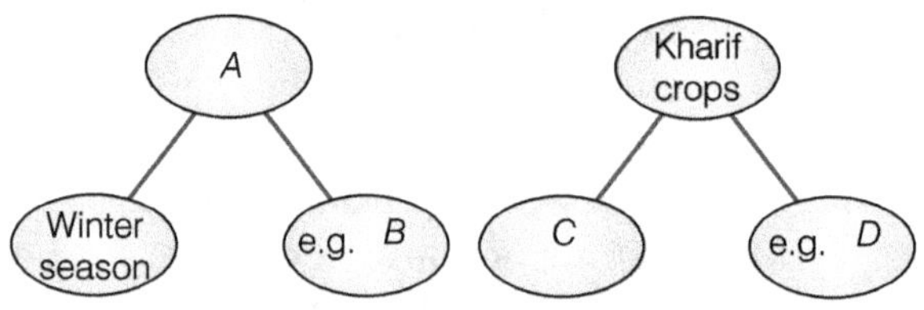

	A	B	C	D
(a)	Rabi	Wheat	Summer season	Rice
(b)	Wheat	Summer season	Rice	Rabi
(c)	Rabi	Summer season	Wheat	Rice
(d)	Wheat	Rabi	Summer season	Rice

19. Three different plants P, Q and R were planted in three different fields as shown below.

Key
$\square - P$
$\triangle - Q$
$\bigcirc - R$

Which of the following crop will grow healthy and give maximum produce?

(a) P (b) Q (c) R (d) P and Q

20. Observe the pictures given below and answer the following question.

Bee   Ground Beetle   Lady bug   Praying mantis   Earthworm

These insects are considered as a farmer's friend because they

  I. feed on growing crops.

  II. bring good luck to farmers.

III. help farmers in agricultural processes.

IV. are predators of different pests.

Codes

(a) I and II   (b) I, II and III   (c) III and IV   (d) II, III and IV

PRACTICE SET 

1. Some animals living in water have streamlined body shapes. This helps to
   (a) store food and fats
   (b) reduce resistance in water
   (c) reduce loss of water
   (d) keep the body warm

2. Why do plants need to disperse their seeds or fruits?
   (a) To make a variety of species
   (b) To maintain their species
   (c) To protect their seeds from being eaten by animals
   (d) To make the species survive in a new place

3. Onions grow from
   (a) bulbs
   (b) tubers
   (c) buds on the leaf margin
   (d) roots

4. As a balloon is filled with water, it expands and increases in weight. This shows that water
   (a) has mass
   (b) occupies space
   (c) is a kind of matter
   (d) All of these

5. Seasons on the Earth are caused mainly because of
   (a) the varying distances between the Earth and the Sun
   (b) the spherical shape of the Earth
   (c) the tilt of the Earth's axis
   (d) the presence of plants and animals

6. Jack was feeling very energetic before he ate a very heavy lunch. However, he felt sleepy immediately after eating the full meal. Why?
   (a) He ate many onions
   (b) His brain diverted most of his energy for digestion
   (c) He did not like the food
   (d) None of the above

7. Which of the following shows the correct order in a food chain?
   (a) Plant → bird → caterpillar
   (b) Caterpillar → plant → bird
   (c) Plant → caterpillar → bird
   (d) Bird → caterpillar → plant

8. People studying earthquakes are called
   (a) Seismologists
   (b) Doctors
   (c) Astrologers
   (d) All of the above

9. The body is able to move because the muscular system works together with .... system.
   (a) respiratory
   (b) skeletal
   (c) digestive
   (d) circulatory

10. Which of these gives us immunity against diseases?
    (a) Injection
    (b) Vaccine
    (c) Tablets
    (d) Syrups

11. Polio is also called
    (a) infantile paralysis
    (b) lockjaw
    (c) hydrophobia
    (d) varicella

12. Which of the following festival is related to farming?
    (a) Bihu
    (b) Pongal
    (c) Onam
    (d) All of these

13. An example of a force in the direction of motion is
    (a) opening a door
    (b) applying brakes suddenly to a moving car
    (c) a batsman hitting a cricket ball
    (d) drawing water form a well

14. Dingtu can lift a weight of 60 kg on the Earth. How much will he be able to lift when on Moon?
    (a) 60 kg   (b) 10 kg
    (c) 360 kg   (d) 120 kg

15. Seeds are dispersed by
    (a) water   (b) explosion of fruits
    (c) wind   (d) All of these

16. The amount of moisture in air is its
    (a) density   (b) pressure
    (c) temperature   (d) humidity

17. A bird and a bat are similar in that they both
    (a) lay eggs   (b) have wings
    (c) have feathers   (d) have beak

18. During the early stages of germination, the seedling gets the food from the
    (a) soil   (b) seed coat
    (c) seed pores   (d) cotyledons

19. Study the following chain:

    Grass → Goat → Jackal → Tiger

    Who among the following can be called as predators (those who kill others for food)?
    (a) Goat   (b) Tiger and Grass
    (c) Jackal and Tiger   (d) Goat and Jackal

20. The species that is threatened with extinction is called
    (a) endangered species (b) rare species
    (c) vulnerable species (d) extinct species

21. A non-biodegradable waste is
    (a) metallic tins   (b) plastic
    (c) polythene   (d) All of these

22. Storm waves are called ……… .
    (a) tsunami (b) wind   (c) air   (d) lava

23. Which of the following statement is incorrect?
    (a) Rabies is caused by the bite of an infected dog.
    (b) Fever can be prevented by vaccination.
    (c) Polio is a viral disease.
    (d) Cholera is caused by bacteria.

24. Which of the following is not a function of the skeleton of a human being?
    (a) It protects the organs
    (b) It protects the soft tissues
    (c) It maintains the shape of the body
    (d) It keeps the temperature of the body constant

25. Force exerted is
    (a) effort   (b) load
    (c) fulcrum   (d) None of these

26. Which of the following is a simple machine?
    (a) Lever   (b) Pulley
    (c) Screw   (d) All of these

27. Object being closer to the source of light results in a larger shadow.
    True /False
    (a) True   (b) False
    (c) Both (a) and (b)   (d) None of these

28. At any given time, different parts of the Earth experience different seasons. Apart from the Earth's revolution around the Sun. Which of these is the reason for this?
    (a) The Earth's rotation
    (b) The elliptical shape of the Earth's orbit
    (c) The presence of the Moon
    (d) The tilt of the Earth's axis of rotation

29. Which of the following statement is true regarding tiger?
(a) A tiger can see ten times better at night than most of us.
(b) Tiger's whiskers help it to move in the dark and find its prey.
(c) Tigers mark their area with their saliva.
(d) All of the above

30. Of the many kinds of snakes found in our country, only four types of snakes are poisonous. These are
(a) *Python*, Worm snake, Viper, Krait
(b) Sea snake, *Python*, Cobra, *Krait*
(c) *Chameleon*, Cobra, Russel's viper, Worm snake
(d) Krait, Russel's viper, Cobra and Saw-scaled viper

31. Which part of the human skeleton protects the heart?
(a) Skull (b) Ribs (c) Backbone (d) Limbs

32. I have many legs, but I cannot fly. Who am I?
(a) Grasshopper   (b) Butterfly
(c) Centipede   (d) Cockroach

33. Chlorine is added to the water in the swimming pools to
(a) sterilise the water (b) clean the water
(c) enhance the water (d) pollute the water

34. A sudden movement of Earth's crust is called
(a) Earthquake   (b) Glacier
(c) Landslide   (d) Adobo

35. If the earthquake occurs, what should you do?
(a) If you are indoors, stay in and get under a desk or a table
(b) If you are outdoors, stay away from trees and buildings
(c) If you are on a beach, leave and find high ground
(d) All of the above

36. Fossil fuels formed over a long period of time because heat and pressure were applied to
(a) Nitrogen mixed in the water
(b) Organisms buried in the ground
(c) Carbon filtered through limestone
(d) Bacteria on top of the mud

37. Coal is formed from
(a) rocks   (b) mountains
(c) animal's matter   (d) vegetable's matter

38. If your diet is deficient in sour fruits, then you are supposed to suffer from
(a) rickets   (b) beri Beri
(c) scurvy   (d) night blindness

39. Movement and actions are controlled by the
(a) lungs   (b) brain
(c) nerves   (d) blood vessels

40. Water present in container P is transferred to container Q as shown in the figure. Which of the following will change for water because of the transfer?

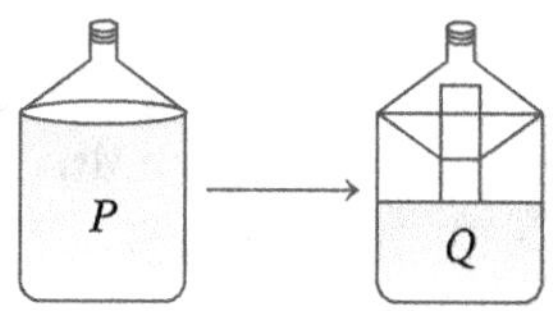

(a) Volume   (b) Mass
(c) Temperature   (d) Shape

41. The flow chart given below represents the change of state of water.

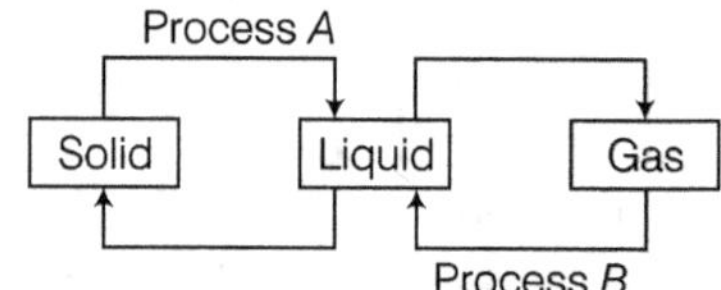

Which of the following represents process *A* and process *B*?

	Process *A*	**Process *B***
(a)	Freezing	Evaporation
(b)	Melting	Condensation
(c)	Freezing	Condensation
(d)	Melting	Evaporation

42. Read the following statements and choose the correct option.

Statement I Plants do not grow well in a greenhouse.

Statement II Gradual increase in global warming will change the Earth's climate for worse.

Statement III Carbon dioxide, water vapours, methane trap solar heat and makes atmosphere warm.

(a) Statement I is incorrect, statements III and II are correct

(b) Statement II is incorrect, statements I and III are correct

(c) Statement III is incorrect, statements I and II are correct

(d) All of the above statements are correct

43. Which level do these organisms occupy in a food chain? Choose the correct option.

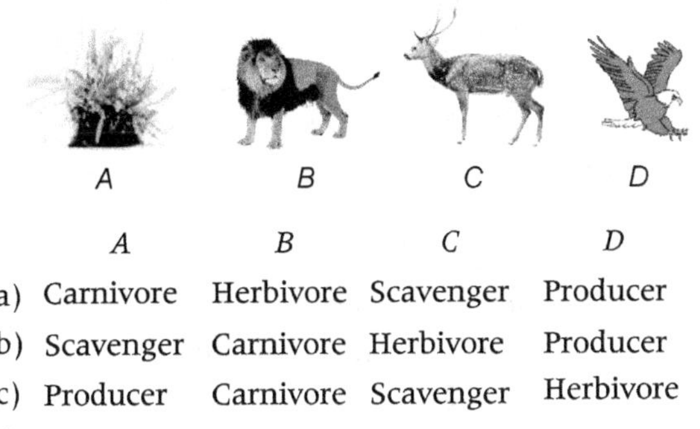

	A	B	C	D
(a)	Carnivore	Herbivore	Scavenger	Producer
(b)	Scavenger	Carnivore	Herbivore	Producer
(c)	Producer	Carnivore	Scavenger	Herbivore
(d)	Producer	Carnivore	Herbivore	Scavenger

44. The diagram below shows a method to purify sea water to get drinking water.

Which of the following processes may have takes place in the above method?

I. Condensation   II. Melting
III. Evaporation   IV. Freezing

Codes

(a) Only I   (b) I and III
(c) II, III and IV (d) All of these

45. The figure given below shows a boy doing fishing.

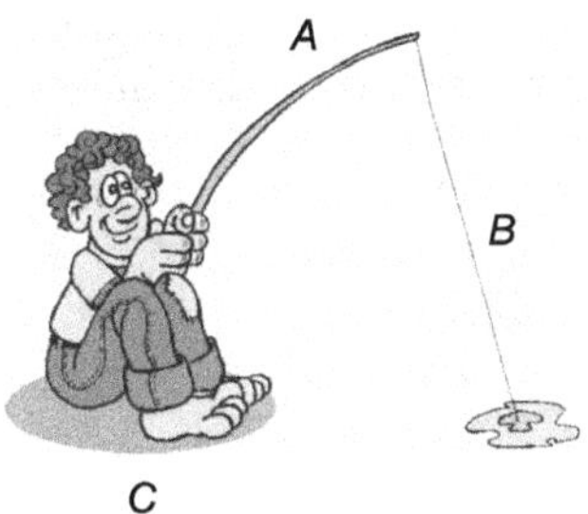

Which of the following options describes the parts of the above figure correctly?

	A	*B*	*C*
(a)	Effort	Load	Fulcrum
(b)	Fulcrum	Load	Effort
(c)	Load	Effort	Fulcrum
(d)	Effort	Fulcrum	Load

46. In an experiment shown below, the sheets *A*, *B* and *C* are arranged in a straight line in a dark room. When the torch is switched on, a bright circular patch of light is seen on the sheet *B* only.

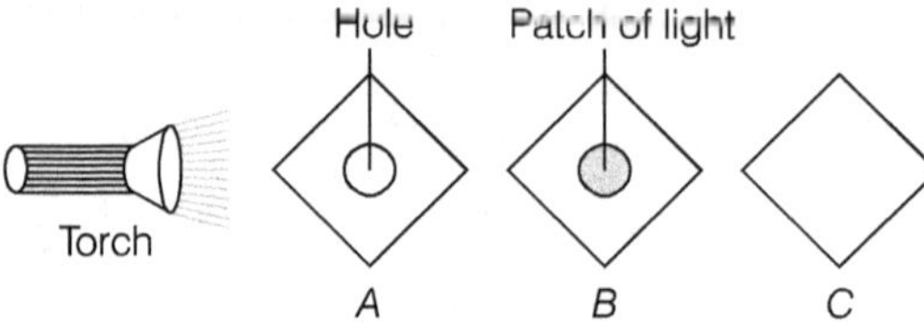

Which of the following materials constitute sheets *A*, *B* and *C* respectively?

	A	*B*	*C*
(a)	Wood	Clear plastic	Rubber
(b)	Rubber	Wood	Clear plastic
(c)	Clear plastic	Rubber	Wood
(d)	Clear plastic	Wood	Rubber

47. Match the following food products with the nutrients they are rich in.

	Column I		Column II
A.		1.	Vitamins
B.		2.	Fat
C.		3.	Carbohydrates
D.		4.	Proteins

Codes

	A	B	C	D
(a)	1	2	3	4
(b)	3	1	2	4
(c)	4	1	3	2
(d)	3	4	1	2

48. Complete the following flow chart with appropriate terms related to respiration in human beings.

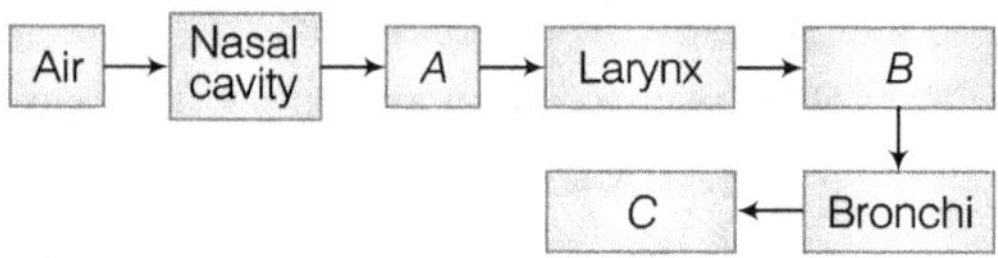

(a) *A*–Alveoli, *B*–Pharynx, *C*–Trachea
(b) *A*–Pharynx, *B*–Trachea, *C*–Alveoli
(c) *A*–Pharynx, *B*–Alveoli, *C*–Trachea
(d) *A*–Alveoli, *B*–Trachea, *C*–Pharynx

49. Path of food through your body is given. Which is the correct sequence?
(a) Mouth → Food pipe → Stomach → Small intestine → Large intestine
(b) Mouth → Stomach → Food pipe → Small intestine → Large intestine
(c) Mouth → Food pipe → Stomach → Large intestine → Small intestine
(d) Mouth → Food pipe → Small intestine → Stomach → Large intestine

50. Salman accidentally touches a hot surface and then quickly pull his hand away, which two systems in the human body were involved with his action and reaction?
(a) Nervous and muscular
(b) Skeletal and circulatory
(c) Nervous and respiratory
(d) Muscular and respiratory

PRACTICE SET 02

1. The organisms given below are similar as they all

   (a) crawl   (b) fly   (c) eat insects
   (d) take care of their young ones

2. Which of the following animals breathe through gills?

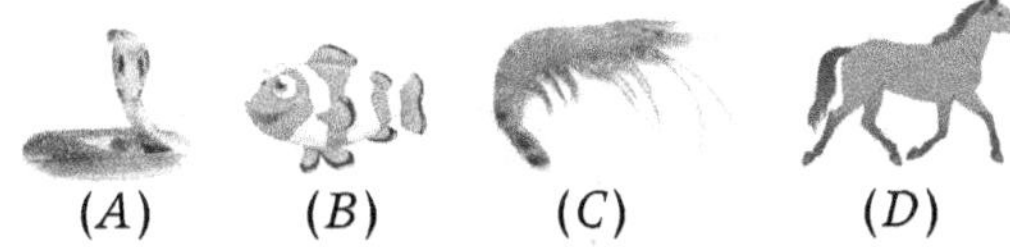

   (A)   (B)   (C)   (D)
   (a) Only *D*   (b) Only *A* and *C*
   (c) Only *B* and *C* (d) Only *A, B* and *C*

3. Where does the food come from when the seed has not grown its leaves?
   (a) From other trees
   (b) From air
   (c) Seed uses its stored food
   (d) From soil

4. From which part of plant can sugarcane be grown?
   (a) Roots   (b) Stems
   (c) Leaves   (d) None of these

5. Heart: Circulatory system :: .... : Nervous system
   (a) Lungs (b) Kidney (c) Bones (d) Brain

6. Vitamins play important role in the functioning of our body. Which vitamin is required for proper vision?
   (a) C   (b) K   (d) E   (d) A

7. A list of important organs of our body is given below. Select the correct option that shows the correct sequence of the location of the organs, from top to bottom of the body.
   Kidneys, lungs, liver, brain
   (a) Kidneys, lungs, liver, brain
   (b) Kidneys, liver, lungs, brain
   (c) Brain, kidneys, lungs, liver
   (d) Brain, Lungs, liver,kidneys, brain

8. Plants produce their own food with the help of water and carbon dioxide. Some plants are carnivores as they trap insects and feed on them. Which of the following is an example of carnivore plant?
   (a) Pitcher plant   (b) Sweet pea
   (c) Chrysanthemum (d) Tulip

9. Which of the following is environment-friendly?
   1. Plastic bottle   2. Paper bag
   3. Diesel   4. Bio-gas
   5. Solar cell
   (a) 1,3 and 4   (b) 2, 4 and 1
   (c) 1 and 3   (d) 2, 4 and 5

10. Which is the smallest bone in the body?
   (a) Incus (b) Maleus (c) Stapes (d) Femur

11. Pick the odd one out.
   (a) Heart   (b) Blood
   (c) Blood vessel   (d) Trachea

12. Which food item provide energy?
   (a) Rice   (b) Sugar
   (c) Bread   (d) All of these

13. Which of the following is a communicable disease?
(a) Typhoid
(b) Dibetes
(c) Obesity
(d) Heart diseases

14. What is the outermost part of tooth called?
(a) Dentine
(b) Enamel
(c) Pulp
(d) None of these

15. Which of the following is a good source of iron?
(a) Butter
(b) Potato
(c) Tomato
(d) Beetroot

16. These living beings give out oxygen and take in carbon dioxide during daytime. Which of the following is being described here?
(a) Trees
(b) Reptiles
(c) Amphibians
(d) Insects

17. This respiratory organ in this insect is not same as the respiratory system in humans. Breathing in this insect occurs through a different system of, respiratory organs.

What is the name of the respiratory organs in this insect?
(a) Gills
(b) Lungs
(c) Spiracles
(d) Stomata

18. A chemical change is a process in which a substance undergoes changes in its chemical properties. Which of the following is a chemical change?
(a) Melting of ice
(b) Boiling of water
(c) Cooking of vegetable
(d) Tearing of newspaper

19. The intensity of an earthquake is measured with
(a) Barometer
(b) Hydrometer
(c) Polygraph
(d) Seismograph

20. If we boil water in a closed system what can we expect to happen to the amount of matter in that system?
(a) It should stay the same
(b) It will increase
(c) It will decrease
(d) It will first increase and then decrease

21. The components of air which are harmful to living beings are
(a) Nitrogen and carbon dioxide
(b) Dust and water vapour
(c) Smoke and water vapour
(d) Dust and smoke

22. Water present in sea and ocean are called
(a) Transparent water
(b) Pure water
(c) Hard water
(d) Soft water

23. Image shown below is

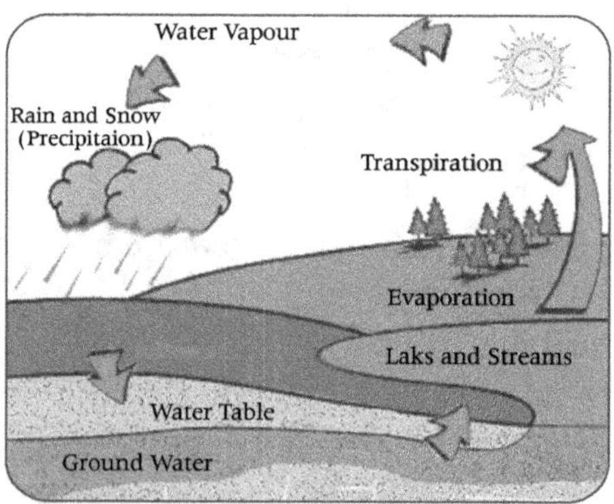

(a) Water change
(b) Water life
(c) Water cycle
(d) Water range

24. The two forms of oxygen found in the atmosphere are
(a) water and ozone
(b) water and oxygen
(c) ozone and oxygen
(d) water and carbon-dioxide

25. Which acid is used in the production of fertilisers?
(a) Nitric acid   (b) Hydrochloric acid
(c) Sulphuric acid   (d) Carbonic acid

26. Kharif crops are harvested in
(a) June - July
(b) October - November
(c) May - June
(d) March - April

27. Match the following columns.

Column I		Column II
A.	Star	1. Satellite
B.	Phases	2. Large blue seas with ice at its ports
C.	Earth	3. A ball of hot glowing gases
D.	Moon	4. Different shapes of moon

Codes

	A	B	C	D		A	B	C	D
(a)	1	3	4	2	(b)	3	4	2	1
(c)	1	2	3	4	(d)	2	3	1	4

28. A planet reflect most of the sunlight it receives. It is also called morning star and evening star. What is the name of the planet?
(a) Mercury   (b) Venus
(c) Jupiter   (d) Saturn

29. Which among the following is not a part of a volcano?
(a) Crater (b) Vent (c) Lava (d) Tidal wave

30. Pick the correct option.
(a) Liquid can freeze (b) Solids can freeze
(c) Gas can freeze   (d) All of these

31. Which among the following is an effect of global warming?
(a) Melting of polar ice caps.
(b) Rise in water levels of oceans.
(c) Flooding of places near the sea.
(d) All of the above

32. Name the process in which clean water is poured into another container without disturbing the sediments.
(a) Sedimentation
(b) Decantation
(c) Evaporation
(d) Filtration

33. Choose the incorrect option.
(a) Car tire - Road - Friction force
(b) Iron - Magnet - Magnetic force
(c) Floating boats - Buoyant force
(d) Ships - Spring force

34. Pick the odd one out.
(a) Bicycle   (b) Pulley
(c) Wedge   (d) Screw

35. The measure of how much material makes up an object is called the
....
(a) volume   (b) weight
(c) mass   (d) matter

36. The list of industrial sources of air pollution and their emissions are given below.

A.	Fossil fuel	1.	Carbon dioxide
B.	Plating	2.	Particulates
C.	Fertilizers	3.	Metal fumes

Codes

	A	B	C
(a)	1	2	3
(b)	3	2	1
(c)	1	3	2
(d)	3	1	2

37. Plants can produce food through photosynthesis with the help of carbon dioxide and water. This process cannot take place without the help of a pigment. Identify the pigment.
(a) Haemoglobin   (b) Chlorophyll
(c) Biliverdin   (d) Carotene

38. Three glasses *A, B* and *C* having equal amount of water were taken at room temperature and equal amount of salt was added to each one of them. After that, *A* was cooled, *B* was heated and *C* was left undisturbed. Water in which glass will now taste most salty?
(a) *A*
(b) *B*
(c) *C*
(d) All will taste the same

39. The given picture shows that air ....

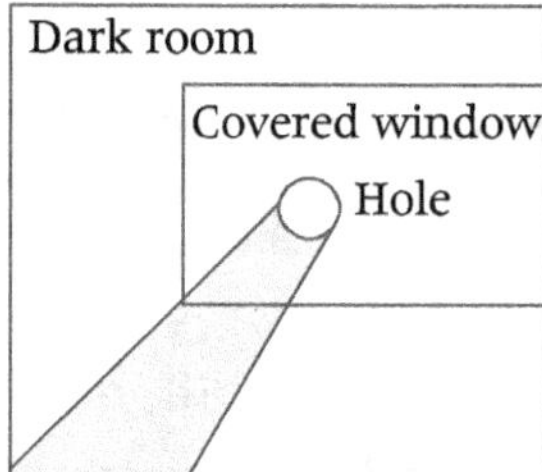

(a) has mass   (b) occupies space
(c) contains dust (d) gives shape to things

40. Name the soft and fatty material found in bones, which help in making red blood cells.
(a) Rib cage   (b) Platelets
(c) Brain   (d) Bone marrow

41. In which of the following processes, condensation has taken place?
I. Wet laundry drying in the Sun.

II. A pot of cold water heating upon a stove.
III. A cloud appearing when the door of the freezer was opened.
IV. Water droplets appearing on the mirror in the bathroom when hot water was turned on.
V. Perspiration disappearing from your forehead when you sit down to rest after playing.

Codes
(a) I and II   (b) III and IV
(c) II, III and V   (d) I, IV and V

42. Four pupils of Mr. Kapoor's made a statement about leaves of plants. Which of them made incorrect statement?
Sahil : Leaves make food for the plant.
Ravi : Leaves absorb water and minerals from the soil.
Amit : Leaves hold the plant firmly in the soil.
Hari : Exchange of gases like carbon dioxide and oxygen occur through leaves.

Codes
(a) Only Sahil   (b) Only Ravi
(c) Ravi and Amit   (d) Sahil and Hari

43. Fill in the blanks using the options given below :
I. Houses of heavy rainfall area have .... roof.
II. People living in Earthquake prone areas prefer to build their houses with .... and ....
III. A house having tin roof remains hot during ....
IV. People of Srinagar generally live in ....

	I	II	III	IV
(a)	no	cement, bricks	winters	tent house
(b)	flat	bricks, cement	winters	Shikara
(c)	sloped	wood, mud	summers	houseboats
(d)	tin	mud, wood	summers	Rebo

44. Varun eats roti and chews it properly. His mother asks him does roti tastes different after chewing for longer time. How does its taste differ?
(a) Yes, it tastes a bit sweeter
(b) No, it tastes the same
(c) Yes, it tastes a bit bitter
(d) Yes, it tastes a bit salty

45. Amar and Neha were hitting benches with small sticks. Neha put her ears on the bench directly and hears the sound much louder. Amar told her that sound travel faster in the medium (bench) than air.
(a) Sound do not need air
(b) Solids are closely packed substances
(c) Liquids can change shape
(d) Solids cannot change shape

46. During lightening and thunder why the sound of thunder appears much later than the appearance of lightening.
(a) Sound travels faster than light
(b) Light travels faster than sound
(c) Sound allows light to appear first
(d) Sound needs medium to propagate

47. Fill in the blanks using suitable words given in the options below:
I. Matter consists of atoms and ....
II. Matter exists in .... states solids, liquids and gases.
III. In mixtures, each constituent material .... its individual properties.
IV. The molecular force of .... in case of gases is very low.
V. .... have fixed shape and volume.

	I	II	III	IV	V
(a)	molecules	four	loses	repulsion	solids
(b)	atom	three	retains	repulsion	liquids
(c)	molecules	three	retains	attraction	solids
(d)	compound	two	loses	attraction	liquids

48. I am a plant with thick leaves, green in colour. I need moisture to grow, I am found on nill station. Who am I ?
(a) Tea   (b) Banana
(c) *Cactus*   (d) Rose

49. Which of the following is not a result of global warming?

(a) Increased chances and intensity of droughts and heat waves

(b) Melting of polar ice

(c) More floods

(d) More trees

50. Goitre is caused by deficiency of .... In it, a gland in the .... region swells. Goitre can be prevented by using iodised salt or by having ....
(a) iodine, facial, leafy vegetables
(b) calcium, neck, seafood
(c) iodine, neck, seafood
(d) iron, neck, fruits

Hints & Solutions

Animals

1. (*b*) Prawns have hard shell called as exoskeleton which protects the inner soft body parts.

2. (*c*) The birds wing is a modified form of forelimbs. The wings give birds the ability to fly.

3. (*a*) The outer part of elephant's ears is bigger than dog and cat's ear, which allow them to perceive or capture faintest sound from the surrounding and give them extreme sense of hearing whereas snakes do not have ears they cannot hear and can just feel the vibration on the ground.

4. (*c*) Part *A* is correctly identified as flippers in penguins. These help the penguins to swim in the water.

5. (*b*) Migration is the movement of large group of animals / birds from their habitat to other places to avoid harsh conditions like extreme cold or heat of their habitat environment.

6. (*d*) Amphibian means living in both land and water. Nearly all amphibians start their life in a larval aquatic stage after hatching from an egg. From there they grow limbs and morph into their adult stage.
e.g. Frog and tortoise.

7. (*d*) Fish lie under water and does not have fur. They have scales on their body.

8. (*c*) Based on feeding habits, animals can be herbivores, carnivores or omnivores. Since elephants are herbivores and snakes are carnivores they can be removed from the row. Cats and dogs are omnivores, they will remain in the row.

9. (*b*) Zebra, bear and lizard have feet to move on the ground. Shark uses their tail and fin to swim under water, whereas caterpillar crawls with the help of their body. Crow flies in the sky with the help of their wings.

10. (*c*) Sloping branches are the feature of trees present in mountain areas. Plants in desert have reduced transpiration and thick stems. Desert plants have small leaves or no leaves. Sometimes, leaves are converted into spine.

11. (*b*) Snail has shell as the outermost body covering which protects the inner body parts from injuries
For other options
- Birds – Feathers – Helps in flight
- Arctic fox – Fur – Keeps the body warm
- Porcupine – Spine – Protects from predators.

12. (*b*) An eagle has a strong eyesight that helps them to notice its prey on the ground, while flying high in the sky.

13. (*a*) Silkworms can smell their females many kilometres away from them. They are the ones who secrete a natural protein fibre which can be woven into silk.

14. (*b*) As tiger's sight is six times better than humans during night, so they can see their prey easily in night and thus can hunt easily.

15. (*a*) Birds have an advantage of having eyes on either side of the head. Eyes on both sides of birds let them focus on two things at the same time.

16. (*b*) Camouflage is the ability of an organism to blend with its surroundings and remain unnoticed by their predators. Since the *Chameleon* is walking on grass, it will change to green colour to blend with the grass.

17. (*c*) In the flow chart, *X* is snail whose body covered by a shell but have no gills, they respire through lungs.
Y is bird their body is covered by feathers which also imparts the ability to take flight in birds.
Z in fish, they have gills for respiration and body is covered by scales.
Hence, option (c) is correct.

18. (*a*) Mosquito can find us by the heat of our body.

19. (*b*) Statement I is false. All birds are not capable of flying. e.g. Ostrich, emu, kiwi, penguins, etc. These are flightless birds.

20. (*b*) Sense of smell allow ants to moves in a line.

Plants

1. (*b*) For vegetative propagation, plant parts like stems, roots and leaves are utilised to produce new plants. These parts contain buds which can grow under favourable conditions.

2. (*c*) The figure represents vegetative propagation of a potato plant.
The new plant is developing from buds on the surface of parent plant.

3. (*c*) Stems of rose plants can grow into new plants.

4. (*c*) The seed used its stored food present in the cotyledons untill the leaves grow.

5. (*a*) Seeds are found in the fruits which are developed from the flowers. The development of the fruit from flower starts from the stage of fertilisation. The result of fertilisation is meant for development of the ovule into the seed.

6. (*b*) In the given diagram, which are future leaves, '*A*' is cotyledons '*B*' is tiny shoot, which develops as main stem and '*C*' is tiny root, which develops as roots of the plant.

7. (*b*) Carbon dioxide and water are required for photosynthesis. Which result in the production of oxygen and glucose. In the given diagram, the arrow indicates the intake of carbon dioxide and water (*X*) by plants. The glucose and oxygen (*Y*) are indicated by the arrows outwards, that means they are produced.

8. (*a*) Four major agents of dispersal of seeds are explosion of plants, wind, water and animals. They transfer the seeds away from parent plant, so they are agents of dispersal of seeds. They are required for the production of new plants.

9. (*d*) The columns can be matched correctly as follows
A. Dispersal is carrying of seeds away from their parent plant.
B. Germination is development of the seed into seedling.
C. Reproduction is the process of production of new plants from parent plants similar to them.

10. (*d*) Pitcher plant is an insectivorous plant that feeds on insects.

11. (*b*) The seed is from *Xanthium* plant. It is dispersed by animal. It is covered with stiff, hooked spines, which are sticky in nature and sticks to animal fur and clothings.

12. (*d*) The correct option for *A, B, C* are water, pea and animals, respectively. Lotus seeds are dispersed by water, pea plant use explosion mechanism for seed dispersal and tigermial seeds are dispersed with the help of animals.

13. (*a*) Statement I and III are false while II and IV are true
   I. Plants bind soil and thus prevent soil erosion.
   II. All the seeds do not grow into a new plant.
   III. Air is required for seeds to breathe.
   IV. Plants are the only producer of food on Earth.

14. (*c*) No growth, is observe as warmth, sunlight and air were absent, which are essential components for germination of seeds. In the absence of these environmental factors, seeds will not germinate.

15. (*b*) Onion and ginger are related to each other as they are underground stems. In both of these new plants grow from stems.

16. (*d*) In set up D, the seed is getting appropriate air, water and light, thus it will germinate. In other set up seed will not germinate because, *A*-lacks moisture, *B* - has excess water, *C* - no conditions for germination are present.

17. (*b*) The correct option for *X* is bamboo, as it yields wood used in construction and fibres used in making bags, etc. whereas *Y* is aloe vera as it is a medicinal plant used to treat a variety of skin and hair ailments.

18. (*d*) The seed leaves of the plant become smaller as the plant grows bigger. This is because the food from the seed leaves are used by plants. Once all the stored food from the cotyledon is used up, then they shed away.

19. (*d*) Tulsi plant has both medicinal as well as religious value.

20. (*b*) Photosynthesis is a process of making food by plants. Pollination refers to transfer of pollen grain from anther to stigma. Scattering of seed is known as seed dispersal and the growth of a baby plant from a seed is called as seed germination.

21. (*b*) When the seeds are sown so much closer to each other, there will be a competition for acquiring the basic requirements like space to grow and spread nutrients, light, etc. As a result most plants will not be able to grow and can die out completely.

Human Body and Its Functioning

1. (*c*) I am a skull a bony cage-like structure whose function is to protect the brain.

2. (*b*) Blinking of eyes does not involve the use of joints.

3. (*c*) In the given relationship, the joint present in knees is hinge joint.

4. (*c*) The part *C* is not matched correctly with its function. *A* is the skull which protects brain; *B* is the ribcage, which protects heart and lungs; *D* is femur, which is the longest bone of our body. But *C* is the pelvic bone, which does not protect our spinal cord rather backbone protects the spinal cord.

5. (*b*) An X-ray gives the details of fracture to the doctor.

6. (*d*) *Q* is the outer ear, which collect sounds from our surroundings and pass them to ear drum.
   P is the middle ear, which amplifies the sound by 10 times and transmit it to inner ear.
   R is the inner ear, which main site of hearing.

7. (*a*) All statements are true except option (a) which can be corrected as
   We should not wash our eyes with hot water rather we should wash them with cold water.

8. (*c*) The main functions performed by our body has specialised organs for them. The correct match of these functions and related organs are
   Digestion – Stomach;   Circulation – Heart
   Excretion – Kidneys ;   Respiration – Lungs

9. (*b*) Giraffe neck is long because their vertebrae are long than ours otherwise number of vertebrae are same. Each vertebra is very long as compared to ours.

10. (*a*) Ball and socket joint enables us to swing our arms.

11. (*b*) Brain is the controlling center of our body.

12. (*d*) Our skin cannot detect the stimulus of light. It can detect the stimulus of heat, cold and pain.

13. (*a*) The muscles can be identified as follows. *A* is diagram of hand in which voluntary muscles are present. *B* is eye in which involuntary muscles are present. *C* is heart in which cardiac muscles are present. *D* is stomach where smooth, involuntary muscles are present.

14. (*a*) When we eat rice, we develop a sweet taste in mouth, while chewing them. This is because rice contains starch, a type of carbohydrate which changes to sugar due to the action of saliva in our mouth.

15. (*b*) *P*-Muscles of legs are voluntary in nature (i.e they are under our control), *Q*-Heart muscles are involuntary and work tirelessly throughout life and *R*-Lungs muscles are not under our control and can take rest for a while.

16. (*c*) There are two lungs and two kidneys in our body. Therefore, these organs are known as paired organs.

17. (*d*) The skull is made up of 22 bones.

18. (*a*) Our digestive system is such that it starts even by hearing or seeing our favourite dish. As a part of the digestive process, saliva is secreted in our mouth. It is an example of reflex action . It is an automatic action.

19. (*a*) The correct sequence of digestion process is given by option (a). Digestion of food starts in mouth, reaches stomach where it is churned more and mixed with gastric juice. In small intestine, food breaks into simple forms by the action of digestive juices. Undigested part is removed as faeces from the body.

Food, Health and Disease

1. (*c*) Fats are nutrients which yields maximum energy on digestion. Among the given options, butter is a fat, hence it is the correct option.

2. (*b*) Five essential components of a balanced diet are carbohydrates, fats, proteins, minerals and vitamins. A diet that contains adequate amount of nutrients is called balance diet.

3. (*d*) Eggs and meat are protein rich foods. Proteins are known as body building nutrients, which help in growth and development of body. Hence, option (d) is correct.

4. (*b*) Bread, potato, sugar, honey, etc., are carbohydrate rich foods. These food when added to our diet gives us energy. This energy is used by body for various activities.

5. (*b*) The deficiency of vitamin-D cause loss of bone density and increased risk of fractures. Vitamin-D is prepared in our body with the help of sunlight.

6. (*b*) The person is suffering from scurvy, which is caused due to the deficiency of vitamin-C. It causes bleeding of gums and swelling of joints.

7. (*d*) Lack of iodine in diet leads to goitre. Iodised salt is a good way to introduce iodine into the body.

8. (*b*) Roughage, i.e. fibres does not get digested but helps in digestion of food and removal of wastes from the body.

9. (*a*) Food that has been cooked should be kept in refrigerators. This is because warm temperature of storage place causes food to spoil faster.

10. (*a*) AIDS damages the immune system and it can pass from one person to another by various means. It is caused by HIV.

11. (*b*) Mr. Veggy is not correct because source of proteins are not just the non-vegetarian food like chicken and eggs rather many vegetarian food stuffs like milk, cheese, pulses, soya can also provide us with a lot of proteins.

12. (*c*) The columns can be correctly matched as follows
A. Water helps in removal of body wastes as urine and sweat.
B. Proteins are essential for growth and muscle building.
C. Vitamins are needed for proper vision, healthy skin and teeth.
D. Minerals are needed in small amounts for proper functioning of body.

13. (*b*) The columns can be correctly matched as follows
A. Night blindness is caused by deficiency of vitamin-A
B. Beri-beri is caused by deficiency of vitamin-B
C. Scurvy is caused by deficiency of vitamin-C
D. Rickets is caused by deficiency of vitamin-D

14. (*c*) Communicable disease can spread from one person to another through air (i.e. sneezing), direct or indirect contact, etc. Ringworm a disease caused by fungus can spread by sharing things of infected person like clothes, socks, shoes, towel, etc.

15. (*a*) Statements I and III are true, other statements II and IV are false because, proteins are essential for muscle growth and body building. Oils and fats are also required along with carbohydrates, they are source of energy.

16. (*b*) Carbohydrates and fats both are energy giving food.

17. (*a*) Measles being a comunicable disease can spread from an infected person and affect other healthy individuals too. Therefore the doctor did not allow Meena to go to school to protect other children.

18. (*c*) The correct options for *A - D* is
A - Protozoan
B - Chickenpox
C - Through contaminated food and water
D - Flu / Common cold / Influenza.

19. (*a*) Eating uncovered food from roadside is not a good eating habit. Roadside foods may have been spoiled by germs from the air and insects such as housefly.

20. (*c*) Covid-19 disease is caused by corona virus.

Water and Its Uses

1. (*b*) Tap water is not a natural source of water. The water which is coming at our houses is stored water. Natural water comes from rain. When rain comes, the water get stored in the Earth's surface which we usually use by using handpumps and wells.

2. (*d*) Rainwater harvesting is a collection of rain water in specially constructed structures and storing it for long term use.

3. (*b*) The steel container will float on the surface of water. It is lighter than the volume of water displaced by it.

4. (*b*) These are evaporation, i.e boiling water to remove soluble impurities and distillation i.e. removing soluble impurities by boiling water, which turns to steam and then condenses to form pure water.

5. (*c*) Sand does not dissolve completely in water, hence it is a water insoluble impurity. Rest options can dissolve completely in water, i.e. they are water soluble.

6. (*a*) Boiling the water (at 100°C) for 10 minutes or more can kill the germs that may be present in water. Chlorination is disinfection of water using small quantity of chlorine gas, which also kills germs present in water.

7. (*c*) Sedimentation is a process in which impure water is allowed to settle, so that impurities are settled on the base and clean water flows above it. This clean water is further treated to obtain pure water.

8. (*a*) Statements I and II give the correct reason for lowering of groundwater.
As Jaya's village is suffering from low rain fall, the level of groundwater is not being replenished. The continuous use of groundwater causes level of water to decrease. The process of evaporation also lowers the level of groundwater gradually.

9. (*c*) The density of mud is greater than water due to which it sinks. Rest all the materials float on water.

10. (*b*) The correct matches are as follows:
Wells are the source of stored groundwater
Glacier is a freshwater body.
Rain is a natural source of water.
Oceans have high salt content.

11. (*c*) The incorrect statement is option (c). Groundwater remains safe from any contamination by human and animal wastes, since it is stored below the ground.

12. (*b*) The lemon will float in glass 1. This is because the salt makes water thicker by increasing its density.

13. (*b*) Alum is a chemical that is used to speed up the process of sedimentation in water treatment plants. Because, alum particles attach themselves to the dirt particles and making them heavier, which causing them to settle at the bottom of the tank.

14. (*d*) Statements I and III are false and they can be corrected as:
Life is not possible on Earth without water.
Water changes into ice when cooled at sufficient temperature.

15. (*b*) Only statement II is incorrect.
An object floats on a liquid if its density is less than that of liquid because we know that
$$\text{Density} = \frac{\text{Mass}}{\text{Volume}}$$
Less density means the object has less mass and hence, it floats.

16. (*b*) The correct order is
Filteration → Boiling → Chlorination
Sedimentation is not a good method on a large scale for water purification as it takes lots of time to settle down.
Distillation method cannot be used as it is used to separate liquids having different boiling points.

17. (*b*) Container II has wider opening due to which the formation of water vapour is maximum. Hence, the rate of evaporation is maximum. As a result, it will contain less quantity of water.

18. (*b*) Cold drinks are filled with carbon dioxide at certain pressure. By shaking the bottle , dissolved carbon dioxide forms bubble in the bottle and these bubbles move upwards bubbles (gas) are lighter than cold drinks (liquid).

19. (*b*) Soluble substances dissolve completely in water leaving nothing behind, e.g. sugar, salt, alcohol, etc. Insoluble substances do not dissolve leave residues behind or remain as such, e.g. chalk powder, oils, nail fillings, etc. Hence, option (b) is correct.

20. (*d*) Water is colourless, odourless and tasteless. Hence, all the options shows that the water source is contaminated or polluted.

21. (*d*) Rainwater harvesting is a technique of collecting and storing rainwater, so that it can be used for various domestic activities like drinking as well as for irrigation of fields. It helps in reducing water scarcity in a natural way. Also, it helps in avoiding groundwater depletion.

Matter and Materials

1. (*d*) Water vapour is a gaseous form of ice and during condensation, water vapours convert into liquid state.

2. (*b*) During winters, the formation of dew drops is the result of condensation of water vapours. The lowering of temperature in winters causes the water vapours in air to condense.

3. (*c*) Glucose is completely soluble in water and it shows soluble property, whereas chalk powder, tea leaves and saw dust are insoluble materials.

4. (*d*) When two or more substances are combined in an indefinite amount, they are called as mixture.

5. (*b*) Block of wood exists in solid state and hence, exhibit highest force of attraction between its particles in comparision to liquid (milk, juice) and gas (air).

6. (*b*) The molecules of solid are very tightly bound, whereas molecules of liquid are loosely bound and molecules of gases are very loosely bound with each other. So, the order will be oxygen, oil and wood.

7. (*b*) The temperature at which water gets converted into water vapour is known as boiling point.

8. (*a*) The statement II is incorrect.
Volume is the amount of space, which is occupied by the body or an object.

9. (*a*) Transparent material is used for making the front glass (wind screen) of a car because transparent materials allow light to completely pass through them.

10. (*b*) Product of two or more substances in a definite amount is known as compound, such as water (H_2O) . Here, the proportion of hydrogen and oxygen will be 2 : 1 in every situation.

11. (*a*) When a substance changes from liquid to gaseous state, it requires energy so that molecules can move further apart.
Hence, the speed of the particles of substance increases.

12. (*c*) Conversion of milk into curd can never be reversed, hence it is a chemical change.
Mixing of salt into sugar, mixing sand and sugar are not chemical change.

13. (*d*) *A* changes its shape when container is tilted which indicates it is liquid. *B* occupies all the space provided in container which indicates it is a gas. *C* neither changes its shape nor occupies whole space provided to it, like *B* when inverted. It indicates *C* is a solid state.

14. (*b*) Flow chart suggests that *A* does not possess mass which depicts that *A* is not a matter. Hence, *A* is a shadow.
Shadow is a reflection of a matter. It is the image formation phenomeon.

15. (*d*) *B* posseses mass and has definite volume hence, it is a liquid. *C* posseses mass but has no definite shape and volume hence, it is a gas. *D* has mass, definite shape and definite volume which indicates *D* is a solid.

16. (*d*) Vapours condense to form solid, solid melts to form liquid, liquid freezes to form solid and solid changes into vapours directly by the process of sublimation.

17. (*d*) Here, the mixture is first filtered which implies some insoluble solid was present in the mixture. In the next step, the solution has undergone evaporation which implies some soluble impurity was present.

18. (*b*) When sugar is dissolved into the water, the total weight of water and sugar remains constant. Sugar occupies the space between water molecules and hence density of water increases.

19. (*c*) Changing the states of matter does not change its mass as amount of matter remains constant. Hence, Charlie's statement is correct.

20. (*c*) Statements I, III, IV and V are false.
    I. Liquids are mobile and have fixed volume. Attraction between the particles of liquid less as compared to solids and hence, liquid changes their shape.
    III. Gases have mass. A matter is a substance which possess mass and occupy space. It also has volume.
    IV. Mixture contains two or more elements in an indefinite manner.
    V. Matter is anything which occupies space and have mass.

Work, Force and Energy

1. (*b*) Push is a type of force which a man applies to make the object move away from himself, while pull is a type of force which a man applies to make the object move towards himself. So, in the given question, figure *A* describes the push force and figure *B* describes the pull force.

2. (*b*) As aluminium is not a magnetic material, so when the block of aluminium (block *B*) is brought near to the magnet, it does not experience any magnetic force and remains stationary.

3. (*b*) A machine is something that makes a work easier to perform. It can have either few or no moving parts. So, a simple machine can be very large and can take a very short duration to perform their task.

4. (*b*) Since, a screw is an inclined plane wrapped over a cylinder and it is also a type of simple machine which can make the work easier to perform. An inclined plane cannot be a screw because screw is made up of inclined plane.

5. (*d*) When the force is applied on the wedge in the downward direction ($\downarrow$), then the log of wood gets separated by applying the force in right-left direction ($\leftarrow\rightarrow$) on the wood.

6. (*d*) Ships–Spring force is the incorrect option because ships also exhibit buoyant force like floating boats.

7. (*b*) Friction is the force that stops us from slipping when we walk.

8. (*d*) While playing, Romeo and Ryan are applying the force in order to throw the ball towards each other.

On applying the force while catching the ball gets slow down and somewhere stopped. In this manner, they are playing their game and all the given options are followed by this activity.

9. (*c*) According to Newton's third law of motion, to every action, their is always an equal and opposite reaction. So, when an electric iron is dropped by Selvi on the floor, then the reaction force is applied on electric iron by the floor.

10. (*d*) While initiating the game, the knot on the rope did not shift at first because both the teams applied an equal force in the opposite directions on the rope, due to which the net force became zero.

11. (*b*) In the given figure, wheel and axle is used instead of pulley and lever. When wheel is rotated, a rod attached with the wheel also rotates. This rod is called axle. A rope is wrapped on the axle and this set up is used for wells to get ground water.

12. (*c*) When Rohit throws the basketball in the upward direction, at this point, the velocity of the basketball is maximum but the moment, it will reach the highest point, its velocity becomes zero and we know that the kinetic energy of the body is characterised by its velocity. So, at the highest point, the kinetic energy of the ball will be zero.

13. (*d*) As we know that, potential energy is characterised by the height of the body. So, ball at *A* possesses maximum potential energy. While according to given figure, the kinetic energy of ball is minimum at maximum height but as it slides down, it starts gaining the velocity and till reaching the lowest points, it becomes maximum, hence kinetic energy becomes maximum at point *D*.

14. (*c*) When the boy starts the car with the help of remote in his hand, then the chemical energy, of the battery is converted into electric energy which is again converted into kinetic energy, which makes the car to move.

15. (*c*) Axle is used in car tyres. They bear the weight of the car and helps to turn the car left and right.
Pulley is used in elevators. Flyovers are inclined plane. Nail cutter is a lever. An axe is a wedge, which is sharp from one side and thick from the other side.

16. (*b*) A. Represents the effort to be applied.
B. Represents the load to be stapled.
C. Represents the fulcrum, which provides the support.

17. (*d*) As shown in the figure, the javelin as a projectile covers a parabolic path from the point *X* to the point *Y*. The gravitational force is acting on the javelin from point *X* to the point *Y*, due to which it remains in air for few seconds and get back to the ground at point *Y*.

18. (*a*) Both the boxes are equally heavy because both the boxes are of 15 kg. But due to the wheels of trolley, there is very less force of friction acting between the wheels and the floor which makes Raghu to pull the box *A* very comfortably. While the force of friction between the box *B* and floor is very high, due to which it is very difficult to pull it.

19. (*d*) Since, in both the set ups, the paper and the steel are non-magnetic material, so when the magnet will move, the box in both the set ups will not move. Secondly, the information regarding the box, it is not given whether the box is magnetic or non-magnetic.

20.

<pre>
            (ii)K
              I
              N
(i)W A T E R
              T
      (iii)O I L
              C
</pre>

(i) (*b*) Hydro means water. When electricity is generated by utilising the energy of falling water, it is called hydroelectricity.

(ii) (*b*) Moving bodies have kinetic energy, thus when we are running we have kinetic energy.

(iii) (*c*) Most machines used for transport use oil as fuel such as petrol and diesel.

Environment and Natural Calamities

1. (*c*) Biotic and abiotic components together form the environment. The biotic components include living things like plants and animals, while the abiotic components include non-living things like soil, air, water and sunlight.

2. (*d*) Chlorofluorocarbons is the gas. It is a very harmful gas, which when released into the atmosphere cause harm to ozone layer. This creates holes in the ozone layer allowing harmful UV rays to pass through and reach the Earth's surface.

3. (*a*) The surrounding factories near the Taj Mahal released harmful gases like SO_2, NO_2, etc., which form acids when they mix with water vapours present in air. This mixture pours down as rain and has caused the white marble of Taj Mahal turn to yellow.

4. (*d*) Burning of dead leaves gives off major pollutants like carbon monoxide. Use of fossil fuels and excessive use of refrigerators gives off chlorofluorocarbons. These pollutants trap sun's heat and cause global warming.

5. (*a*) Waste materials which can be broken down or decompose naturally do not cause soil pollution.
Such materials are called as biodegradable wastes, e.g. fruit peels and paper, wood, clothes, etc.

6. (*b*) The point under the ground, where an earthquake begins is called as the focus.

7. (*c*) Mt Fuji is a volcano that has not erupted in the last 10,000 years but may erupt in future. Such volcanoes are called as dormant or sleeping volcanoes.

8. (*a*) An erupting volcano may trigger natural calamities like cyclones, tsunamis, earthquakes, storms and rock falls.

9. (*a*) Tsunami occurs in water bodies. It is a huge sea or tidal waves caused by under water earthquakes of volcanic eruptions.

10. (*c*) The correct matches are as follows;
Extinct volcano (which can no longer erupt) is Mt Kilimanjaro.
Epicentre is the location just above the focus on Earth's surface.
Cyclones are strong, fast spinning winds formed over water surface.
Greenhouse gases trap the heat from Sun on Earth's surface. They are CO_2, methane, water vapours, etc.

11. (*a*) Statement I is correct. Global warming is considered as an adverse effect of air pollution. This is because the increase in temperature of earth's surface will cause the polar regions to melt. This will cause a rise in level of water in sea and oceans and flooding of surrounding areas.

12. (*c*) The layer of algae which grows on the surface of water reduces the amount of light and fresh oxygen to the plants. This results in death of the plants as they cannot carry out process that are important for their survival.

13. (*c*) Wastes should not be dumped directly into the water bodies. They should be first treated and then only be disposed off into water bodies, so that water bodies do not get polluted.

14. (*a*) The effects of global warming are irreversible. To control these effects it may take us several decades. For example, rise of ocean and sea level are irreversible.

15. (*b*) The car became a greenhosue.
The Sun's heat which enters in the car by glass windows is not allowed to escape. Thus, it increased the temperature inside the car. Level of CO_2. It is almost similar to the greenhouses.

16. (*d*) Category I materials are all biodegradable, i.e. they can decompose naturally while those in category II are non-biodegradable. These materials pollute our environment for a long time, hence should be recycled.

17. (*b*) Statement II is true. For false statements the correct forms are
Earthquake with an intensity of 7-8 richter causes massive destruction of life and property.
Damage to ozone layer is caused by chlorofluorocarbons.
Drinking contaminated water can cause diseases like cholera, typhoid, diarrhoea, dysentry, etc.

18. (*b*) The disaster is an earthquake. It is better to hide beneath tables and desks rather than running in crowded place during earthquakes.

Natural Resources

1. (*a*) X is oxygen (21%). It is the part of air which is used by human beings and animals for breathing.

2. (*c*) Stratosphere is the ozone containing layer of atmosphere. Ozone filters the sunlight that pass through it and stops harmful UV rays therefore it protects the living organisms from harm that can be caused by UV rays.

3. (*b*) Since air supports burning, so the candle will extinguish. This happens because the glass stops the entry of air from outside, this causes the candle to stop burning after it uses the air present inside the glass.

4. (*c*) The pot *B* where Aditya used loamy soil. This is because loam can hold moisture very well has good level of nutrients and organic matter. It is thus suited for plant growth.

5. (*b*) Marble, which is a six letter word and is found in variety of colours. It is made up of limestone.

6. (*b*) Pumice, a type of igneous rock is used as a body scrubber. Rest other statements are correct.

7. (*d*) Due to deforestation more water will flow away carrying along with the topsoil layer leading to soil erosion.

8. (*c*) Sedimentary rocks are formed from broken pieces of old rocks, e.g. Shale.
   Igneous rocks are formed due to cooling of molten lava or magma, e.g. Granite.
   Metamorphic rocks are formed by high heat and pressure, e.g. Quartzite.

9. (*b*) Student II is correct. This experiment shows that air has weight. As soon as the balloon on one side is pricked, it become lighter and went upwards, while air filled balloon went downwards.

10. (*b*) If farmers leave their soil in the absence of any plants and their roots, soil becomes loose and is susceptible to be carried away by wind or water. This may result into loss of fertility of soil. So, by growing cover crops they try to keep their soil intact and prevent soil erosion.

11. (*b*) *X* is weathering, i.e. the breaking of rocks into smaller particles to form soil, while *Y* could be any activity that results in erosion of soil, i.e. cutting of trees (deforestation) overgrazing by animals, etc.

12. (*a*) Rock *X* is limestone, formed from shells and skeletons of small sea animals. It is a sedimentary rock.

13. (*a*) We need to conserve fossil fuel because they take millions of years to form. If we use them recklessly then we will not have them for our future use. Moreover they also pollute the environment by releasing harmful gases, when burnt. So, we should use them properly.

14. (*c*) It is known as terrace farming and practised only in mountains or hilly regions to prevent erosion of top soil due to water.

15. (*d*) Statement II and III are false, because there are many human factors, which are responsible for soil erosion, like deforestation, etc. As a result of soil erosion the land loses its fertility.

16. (*a*) Air has mainly oxygen, nitrogen, carbon dioxide. Oxygen is used for burning, carbon dioxide is used by plants for breathing and nitrogen present in air is used by plants indirectly (through microorganisms) to prepare food.

17. (*b*) Pot *B* will lose more soil because there are no roots of plants, which can bind the soil and prevent it from eroding away.

18. (*b*) Rocks are different in shape and sizes. They also vary in their colours. Minerals are uniform in their colour and shape. They are pure and have fixed compositions.

19. (*c*) Once the remains of plants and trees were there on soil. Then mud and stones covered that eventually. Due to their weight and pressure they turned slowly into a soft rock. If they are not disturbed for years then due to the heat and pressure of Earth these soft rocks become hard rocks, which is coal. So, the correct sequence of formation of coal is
$$II \rightarrow IV \rightarrow III \rightarrow I$$

20. (*d*) Statement III is incorrect but statements I and II are correct. Statement III can be corrected as: Slate is a form of metamorphic rock.

Our Universe

1. (*b*) Group of stars joined to form different patterns in the sky are called constellation.

2. (*d*) The Earth consist of three layers, the outer layer is called crust, middle layer is called mantal and the innermost layer is called core.

3. (*b*) The Moon and stars are not visible during day. The Sun is too bright during the day due to which Moon and stars become less visible.

4. (*c*) The movement of the Earth at its fixed axis is known as rotation. These rotations are responsible for change in day and night.

5. (*a*) A. Pluto is considered to be as dwarf planet because it is the smallest in size among all the planets.
   B. Mars is known as the red planet because it appears in the sky as an orange-red star.
   C. In the solar system, Jupiter is the largest planet.
   D. Venus is known as the brightest planet because its thick clouds reflect most of the sunlight that reaches it.
   E. Earth is known as the blue planet. It is because 75% of earth is covered with water.

6. (*d*) All the options are correct except (d) because the Moon is near to Earth but it is not a star. Moon is a natural satellite which revolve around the Earth.

7. (*d*) On unscrambling, we get 3 constellation namely URSA MAJOR, ORION and CASSIOPEIA.

8. (*d*) *X* - Arun, *Y* - Varun
in hindi Uranus is called Arun and Neptune is called Varun.

9. (*c*) The figure given above shows the lunar eclipse which comes into play when Moon passes directly behind the Earth and with the Earth in the middle. Hence, a lunar eclipse can only occur at the night of a full Moon.

10. (*c*) Asteroids lie or reside between Jupiter and Mars and according to the order of planets in solar system, planet *X* is Jupiter and planet *Y* is Mars.

11. (*b*) It is mandatory to carry oxygen in gas cylinders to travel in outer space. It is because there is no air in space. So, in order to breathe, the space traveller are required to carry the oxygen gas cylinder with them, else they will not be able to survive.

12. (*b*) Option (b) best defines the position of the Earth, Moon and Sun which represents a solar eclipse. In this eclipse, the Moon passes between the Sun and the Earth. This can happen only at the new Moon.

13. (*b*) In the areas between the two high tides, the water form the low tides. The intensity of the tides vary with the phases of the Moon.

14. (*c*) Among the given options, option (c) will be correct. It is because Aryabhatta was the first Indian satellite launched in 1975.

15. (*c*) Saturn is the 2nd largest planet. It has 7 rings made up of ice, dust and rock. It is the sixth planet of solar system.

16. (*c*) Since, our solar system consists of 8 planets and Sun. All these planets revolve around the Sun throughout the year. They shine brightly by the sunlight reflected by them.

17. (*c*) Sun is the source of energy in our solar system, Saturn is the most beautiful planet because of its ring. Asteroids are rocky objects revolving around the Sun in an orbit. Venus has thick clouds which reflects most of sunlight and hence, it is the most brightest planet of the solar system. Pluto is not a planet anymore. It is called a dwarf planet.

18. (*d*) Jupiter is the largest planet of the solar system having rings around him.
Earth is the only planet which has oxygen water and atmosphere. Earth is called as blue planet as it is covered with water.

19. (*c*) *P*–Sun is a part of solar system, but it do not revolve.
Q–Venus is called as the evening and morning star.
R–Neptune is the farthest planet in the solar system.

20. (*d*) Sohan and Mohan are correct, while Akhil and Anuj made the false statement because Jupiter has more than 50 Moons and Mars has 2 moons as its natural satellite.

Farming and Agriculture

1. (*c*) The production of crop plants at a large scale is known as agriculture.

2. (*b*) Maize is a five letter word and commonly known as 'corn' and grows in summer season. It grows well in dry soil of plains and hills.

3. (*d*) Kharif crops like paddy (Rice) require a large quantity of water that is why monsoon season with low light and moderate temperature (25-27°C) is perfect for its cultivation.
Rice crops can also withstand water logging conditions that occur commonly during this season.

4. (*c*) The figure depicts the process of ploughing of an agricultural field. This process helps in loosening the soil before sowing. As a result the soil gets aerated and nutrients get mixed properly.

5. (*d*) The crops which are sown at the arrival of monsoon season (June-October) are called as Kharif crops. All the crops mentioned are Kharif crops.

6. (*b*) Option (b) is incorrect. It can be corrected as
Irrigation–adding water to fields.

7. (*d*) Transplanting or replanting is the technique of moving a plant from one location to another. By transplanting farmers select healthy sapling and plant them at proper distance which increases crop production.

8. (*d*) The seeds should not be sown very deep in the soil. This will make it very difficult for them to receive air, water, nutrients, etc. As a result they can die out. Rest other statements are true.

9. (*c*) The figure represents the process of harvesting, i.e. cutting down the matured crop from field.

10. (*d*) Both of these if used in high concentration on the crops, can cause harm to the crop.

11. (*c*) Neem leaves are insect repellants, i.e. they repel insects away. While storing the grain, insects like cockroaches, locusts, etc. can start eating grains.
The smell of neem leaves will drive them away and keep the grains safe.

12. (*c*) Process *A* is threshing. Post harvest grains are separated manually from their stalks by beating them against a hard surface.
Process *B* is winnowing which separates grain from the chaff using the flow of wind.

13. (*b*) The correct matches are as follows

Wheat, rice, maize, etc.	Food grain crops
Mustard, sunflower, etc.	Oil rich crops
Tea, coffee, etc.	Plantation crops
Cotton	Fibre crop

14. (*a*) The correct order of steps in agriculture are as follows

Ploughing ⟶ Manuring ⟶ Sowing

Winnowing ⟵ Harvesting

15. (*a*) Pulses are legume plants. These plants have the ability to increase the level of nutrients particularly nitrogen in the soil.

16. (*c*) Crops are needed to be protected against grazing animals like cows and goats, pests like locust, grasshopper and diseases. Air and warmth are essential along with water for proper germination of seed and hence growth of plant.

17. (*b*) The small plants growing around the main crops are called weeds. These causes overcrowding on the field and affects the growth of crops. Thus, farmers keep a check on their growth and remove them often.

18. (*a*) '*A*' is Rabi crops. These crops are grown in winter season. '*B*' is an example of Rabi crops, which is wheat. '*C*' is summer season in which Kharif crops are grown.
'*D*' example of such crop is rice.

19. (*b*) Crop *Q* will give maximum yield. This is because the seeds are sown at a uniform distance which will benefit the crops. While, crop *P* and *R* are not uniformly spaced, they will face problem while growing.

20. (*c*) The insects shown are beneficial for farmers because they help in biological control of pest, soil formation, nutrient exchange, etc.
For example, lady bug, beetles, preys on pests that destroy crops, earthworm enhances soil quality, moisture level, etc.

Practice Set 1

1. (*b*)	**2.** (*d*)	**3.** (*a*)	**4.** (*d*)	**5.** (*c*)
6. (*b*)	**7.** (*c*)	**8.** (*a*)	**9.** (*b*)	**10.** (*b*)
11. (*a*)	**12.** (*d*)	**13.** (*c*)	**14.** (*b*)	**15.** (*d*)
16. (*d*)	**17.** (*b*)	**18.** (*d*)	**19.** (*c*)	**20.** (*a*)
21. (*d*)	**22.** (*a*)	**23.** (*b*)	**24.** (*d*)	**25.** (*a*)
26. (*d*)	**27.** (*a*)	**28.** (*d*)	**29.** (*d*)	**30.** (*d*)
31. (*b*)	**32.** (*c*)	**33.** (*a*)	**34.** (*a*)	**35.** (*d*)
36. (*b*)	**37.** (*d*)	**38.** (*c*)	**39.** (*b*)	**40.** (*d*)
41. (*b*)	**42.** (*a*)	**43.** (*d*)	**44.** (*b*)	**45.** (*a*)
46. (*b*)	**47.** (*d*)	**48.** (*b*)	**49.** (*a*)	**50.** (*a*)

Practice Set 2

1. (*b*)	**2.** (*c*)	**3.** (*c*)	**4.** (*b*)	**5.** (*d*)
6. (*d*)	**7.** (*d*)	**8.** (*a*)	**9.** (*d*)	**10.** (*c*)
11. (*d*)	**12.** (*d*)	**13.** (*a*)	**14.** (*b*)	**15.** (*d*)
16. (*a*)	**17.** (*c*)	**18.** (*c*)	**19.** (*d*)	**20.** (*a*)
21. (*d*)	**22.** (*c*)	**23.** (*c*)	**24.** (*c*)	**25.** (*a*)
26. (*b*)	**27.** (*b*)	**28.** (*b*)	**29.** (*d*)	**30.** (*a*)
31. (*d*)	**32.** (*b*)	**33.** (*d*)	**34.** (*a*)	**35.** (*c*)
36. (*c*)	**37.** (*b*)	**38.** (*b*)	**39.** (*c*)	**40.** (*d*)
41. (*b*)	**42.** (*c*)	**43.** (*c*)	**44.** (*a*)	**45.** (*b*)
46. (*b*)	**47.** (*c*)	**48.** (*a*)	**49.** (*d*)	**50.** (*c*)